Lee Canter's

Assertive Discipline®

Secondary Workbook

Grades 9-12

A Publication of Canter & Associates, Inc.

Staff Writer
Marcia Shank

Editorial Staff
Marlene Canter
Jacqui Hook
Patricia Sarka
Kathy Winberry

Design/Graphics
Bob Winberry

©1992 Canter & Associates, Inc.
P.O. Box 2113, Santa Monica, CA 90407-2113
800-262-4347   310-395-3221
www.canter.net

Printed in the United States of America
First printing July 1992
02 01 00   11 10 9 8 7 6

ISBN 0-939007-50-9

PD4170

Contents

INTRODUCTION 4

SECTION ONE: **Your Classroom Discipline Plan**

What Is a Classroom Discipline Plan? 6

Creating Your Classroom Discipline Plan—Rules 8

Creating Your Classroom Discipline Plan—Positive Recognition 12

Creating Your Classroom Discipline Plan—Consequences 47

SECTION TWO: **Launching Your Classroom Discipline Plan**

Talk to Your Administrator About Your Classroom Discipline Plan 58

Teach Your Classroom Discipline Plan to Your Students 60

Send Home a Copy of Your Discipline Plan to Parents 75

SECTION THREE: **Teaching Responsible Behavior**

Determining and Teaching Specific Directions 80

Using Positive Recognition to Motivate Students to Behave 92

Redirecting Non-disruptive Off-task Behavior 98

Implementing Consequences 104

SECTION FOUR: **Difficult Students**

One-to-One Problem-Solving Conferences 110

Using Positive Support to Build Positive Relationships 113

Developing an Individualized Behavior Plan 121

Getting the Support You Need from Parents and Administrators 124

Introduction

Lee Canter's Assertive Discipline has been a highly regarded classroom behavior management program for over 15 years. In 1992 the program was revised to more comprehensively meet the needs of today's classrooms. The focus of the new Assertive Discipline is on teaching students responsible behavior. With this proactive and preventive approach, teachers can go beyond establishing basic discipline in their classrooms to creating learning environments in which students learn to choose appropriate, responsible behavior.

This *Assertive Discipline Secondary Workbook* is your guide to implementing the revised Assertive Discipline program. The easy-to-follow format is concise and practical. Brief overviews of the program's key points are followed by the reproducible forms, positive notes, bookmarks, coupons, raffle tickets tracking sheets, communication and documentation pages, and visual aids that will allow you to successfully integrate the program into your teaching routine.

For a comprehensive understanding of the revised Assertive Discipline program, please read *Assertive Discipline—Positive Behavior Management for Today's Classroom.*

Positive Behavior Management and the Secondary Classroom

Being a teacher is a challenging job—especially in today's world. You may find, like many teachers today, that it is increasingly difficult to establish a classroom environment free from disruptive behavior.

But in spite of the difficulties you face, you *can* create and maintain the kind of classroom in which you can effectively teach and your students can learn and grow academically and socially.

How can you achieve this? By becoming an assertive teacher—an empowered teacher—a teacher of influence. Whatever the age of your students, they will behave more responsibly and have more success in school if you follow these guidelines:

• Establish rules and specific directions that clearly define the limits of acceptable and unacceptable student behavior.

• Teach your students to consistently follow these rules and directions, and to choose to behave responsibly, at all times when they are in your classroom.

• Provide students with consistent positive encouragement and recognition when they do behave. Adolescents are eager for your positive words of encouragement and praise, even if they can't always show it.

• Adopt a positive, assertive manner when responding to students. Students trust and respect the calm, consistent and caring presence of an assertive teacher. They know that the teacher has set limits and that he or she will follow through appropriately whenever a student chooses not to behave. There is no confusion, no second-guessing, no hostility or anger.

• Remember to ask parents and administrators for their assistance when their support is needed. You can't do it alone. Education is a cooperative effort between teacher, student, parents and administration. Rely on each other for the positive assistance you can give.

___

Help your students make the most of their high school years. Create an atmosphere in which student self-esteem can flourish and you can feel accomplished at the end of every teaching day. Become a positive, proactive, assertive teacher—today!

Your Classroom Discipline Plan

In this section of the *Assertive Discipline Secondary Workbook* we will first look at the classroom discipline plan—what it is and how it empowers secondary-level students to become responsible for their behavior choices. Then you will develop a discipline plan for your own classroom with rules, postives and consequences that best fits your needs, and the needs of your students.

Also included in this section is a wide variety of reproducibles that will help you successfully develop and implement your classroom discipline plan.

What Is a Classroom Discipline Plan?

A classroom discipline plan is a system that allows you to communicate the behaviors you expect from students and what they can expect from you in return. The plan provides a framework around which all of your classroom behavior management efforts can be organized.

The goal of a classroom discipline plan is to have a fair and consistent way to establish a safe, orderly, positive classroom environment in which you can teach and students can learn.

A classroom discipline plan consists of three parts:

- RULES that students must follow at all times.

- POSITIVE RECOGNITION that students will receive for following the rules.

- CONSEQUENCES that result when students choose not to follow the rules.

If secondary students are to learn the self-discipline that is so crucial to their success in school, and to their success in life, they first must understand exactly what is expected of them.

Look at it this way: In the workplace, employees are given precise job descriptions and clear explanations of all policies that effect their performance. Only if expectations are clarified can performance be fairly and accurately evaluated.

It is important, therefore, to have a classroom management structure in place that clearly indicates limits and boundaries.

On the following page are four reasons why a classroom discipline plan will help you create a positive learning environment in your classroom that benefits both you and your students.

Sample Classroom Discipline Plan

C L A S S R O O M   R U L E S
Follow directions.
Keep hands, feet and objects to yourself.
No swearing, teasing, name calling or put-downs.
Be in your seat when the bell rings.
Bring required materials to class.

P O S I T I V E   R E C O G N I T I O N
Praise
Positive notes sent home to parents
Positive notes to students
Positive phone calls to students and parents

Additional positives may include:
Coupons for student store
Select own seat for the day
No-homework pass
Coupons and raffle tickets

C O N S E Q U E N C E S

First time a student	
breaks a rule:	Warning
Second time:	Stay in class 1 minute after the bell
Third time:	Stay in class 2 minutes after the bell
Fourth time:	Teacher calls parents
Fifth time:	Send to principal
Severe Clause:	Send to dean

Benefits of a Classroom Discipline Plan

1 A discipline plan makes managing student behavior easier.

Planning is the key to successful classroom management. When you have a plan for how you will respond to student behavior you won't have to make difficult on-the-spot decisions about what to do when a student misbehaves—or how to properly recognize a student who does behave appropriately. You'll know what to do, your students will know what to expect, and the guesswork (and a lot of stress) will be eliminated from your daily disciplinary efforts.

2 A discipline plan protects students' rights.

All students have the right to the same due process in the classroom. A discipline plan will help ensure that you deal with each student in a fair and consistent manner—a fact that plays into the high school student's sense of fairness.

Likewise, the classroom discipline plan protects students' right to learn. Most high school students want to learn and hate having their time wasted by a few.

3 A discipline plan helps ensure safety for all students in the classroom.

Consistently used as part of a teacher's behavior management efforts, a classroom discipline plan helps reduce behavior problems in class. And reduced behavior problems means a safer environment for all students. This is extremely important. Secondary students do not want to be placed in the position of having the "tough" kids running the class.

4 A discipline plan helps ensure parental support.

When you communicate your discipline plan to parents (see pages 75-76), you are letting them know that you care about guiding their children toward making responsible behavioral choices. This is a powerful message of support and professionalism to give to parents.

5 A discipline plan helps ensure administrator support.

A discipline plan demonstrates to your administrator (dean, counselor, principal or vice principal) that you have a well thought-out course of action for managing student behavior in your classroom. When your administrator understands the commitment you've made to effective classroom management, you will be better able to get support when you need it.

It's Your Turn

Now we'll take you through the steps for creating a classroom discipline plan tailor-made for you and your students.

First, you will plan the general rules for your classroom.

Second, you will choose the positive recognition you will use to motivate students to follow those rules.

Finally, you will learn how to most effectively select and use consequences when students choose not to follow the rules.

Option: Form a Behavior Management Team

To best meet the needs of your students, and to minimize confusion over varying expectations from teacher to teacher, collaborate with a few other teachers to develop a common classroom discipline plan. Form a Behavior Management Team with several teachers in your wing or teachers who teach some of the same students you teach (for example, you may all teach ninth-grade subjects). Students will become more cooperative as they find that expectations are consistent from classroom to classroom. The more consistency provided within the school, the easier your job will be.

After formulating the plan, meet with your team once or twice during the quarter or semester to evaluate the effectiveness of the plan and make any changes necessary.

Creating Your Classroom Discipline Plan
Rules

Teachers at the secondary level sometimes assume that students automatically should know how to behave in the classroom. They expect that after six years of elementary school and three years of middle school, a student should understand the general expectations of the classroom.

This assumption is often erroneous. Whether ninth-graders or twelfth-graders, your students all share something in common when they arrive in your class—each brings a variety of behavioral expectations from home and a variety of behavioral expectations from previous teachers and schools.

In addition, different teaching styles and curriculum needs result in different behavioral expectations in high school classes.

Your students can't be expected to know how *you* want them to behave in your classroom unless you make those expectations clear to them. General classroom rules, therefore, are the first part of your classroom discipline plan.

What are general classroom rules?

General classroom rules are those rules that are in place all period long—throughout any activities that might take place. General classroom rules are important because they let all of your students know what basic behavioral expectations you have at all times.

These guidelines will help you choose appropriate rules:

• Choose rules that are observable.
Address behaviors that you can clearly see. Vaguely stated expectations may mean one thing to one student, and an entirely different thing to another. As a result, they often cause

problems by opening the door to arguments regarding interpretation.

For example:

Observable Rules
Keep hands and feet to yourself.

Be in your seat when the bell rings.

No yelling or screaming.

Vague Expectations
Respect teacher and fellow students.

No fooling around when class starts.

No unnecessary talking.

• Choose rules that apply throughout the entire period.
General classroom rules are basic rules that apply all period, no matter what activity is taking place. These are rules that students are expected to follow at all times.

• Choose a limited number of classroom rules.
Three to five general classroom rules are plenty. The more rules you have, the more difficult it will be for students to remember them. Choose the ones you most need so that you can teach and your students can learn.

Now, before you choose your own rules, take a look at some rules that are *not* appropriate general classroom rules. Though often seen in classrooms, we have found that these rules are not appropriate general rules because they are not applicable throughout the period.

Notice that while each rule *sounds* sensible, it cannot be a realistic ongoing expectation.

Rules to Avoid:

- Raise your hand and wait to be called upon before you speak.

Realistically, there are going to be times when students may be *expected* to speak out (for example, in learning groups or occasionally during a class discussion). Also, you may not want to put yourself in the position of having to provide a consequence for what might be simply a student's overly enthusiastic behavior.

- Stay in your seat unless you have permission to get up.

There may be many times during the period when it's OK for a student to get up without asking permission. Again, this rule may not be enforceable throughout the class period.

- Complete all homework assignments.

This rule does not relate to classroom behavior. Also, there may be times when completing homework is out of a student's control.

When you establish general classroom rules that do not clearly reflect your *consistent* expectations, you run the risk of confusing students, and you will not be able to enforce these rules with consistency.

Here are some general classroom rules that are appropriate for grades 9-12.

Notice that each of these rules is applicable every day—throughout the entire class period.

Notice that each one is observable.

- Follow directions.
- Keep hands, feet and objects to yourself.
- Do not leave the room without permission.
- No swearing, teasing or yelling.
- Bring all appropriate materials to class.
- Be in your seat when the bell rings.
- Don't interrupt when someone else is speaking.

Involve students in choosing rules for the classroom.

Many teachers find it beneficial to involve their students in choosing the general rules for the classroom. You might begin by presenting an analogy that helps explain why clearly defined rules are a smart idea: What if driving laws (rules) simply consisted of the admonition to "drive friendly?" What would be the effect in comparison to having clear-cut, carefully spelled-out laws?

Then, during a brief class discussion, ask students to consider how other students sometimes make it difficult for them to pay attention and learn in class. Ask for suggestions for rules that might make it easier to learn.

During the discussion, guide students so that suggested rules are both appropriate and realistic. Consider student input, but be sure that the final rules you choose follow the guidelines given and also follow your own needs as a teacher.

By including students in the process of choosing rules, you will give them ownership in the classroom discipline plan. They will see the classroom rules as their rules (with a rationale that makes sense to them) and will be more motivated to support and remind each other about following the rules.

It's Your Turn

Use the Classroom Rules Worksheet on the next page to plan the general rules you will use in your own classroom. When you're finished, write your rules on the Classroom Rules poster on page 11. Tuck the finished poster away with your supplies. You'll be using it when you introduce your classroom discipline plan to your students.

CLASSROOM RULES WORKSHEET

Use this worksheet to plan your own general classroom rules. We've started the list for you with the rule, "Follow directions." This is an important rule because students must be expected to follow any direction you might give during the day. When choosing the rest of your rules, remember: 1) Rules must be observable, 2) Rules must apply throughout the entire day, and 3) Rules must reflect your teaching style and educational philosophy.

Classroom Rule: Follow directions.

This is an appropriate general classroom rule because:

_____

_____

_____

_____

Classroom Rule: _____

This is an appropriate general classroom rule because:

_____

_____

_____

_____

Classroom Rule: _____

This is an appropriate general classroom rule because:

_____

_____

_____

_____

Classroom Rule: _____

This is an appropriate general classroom rule because:

_____

_____

_____

_____

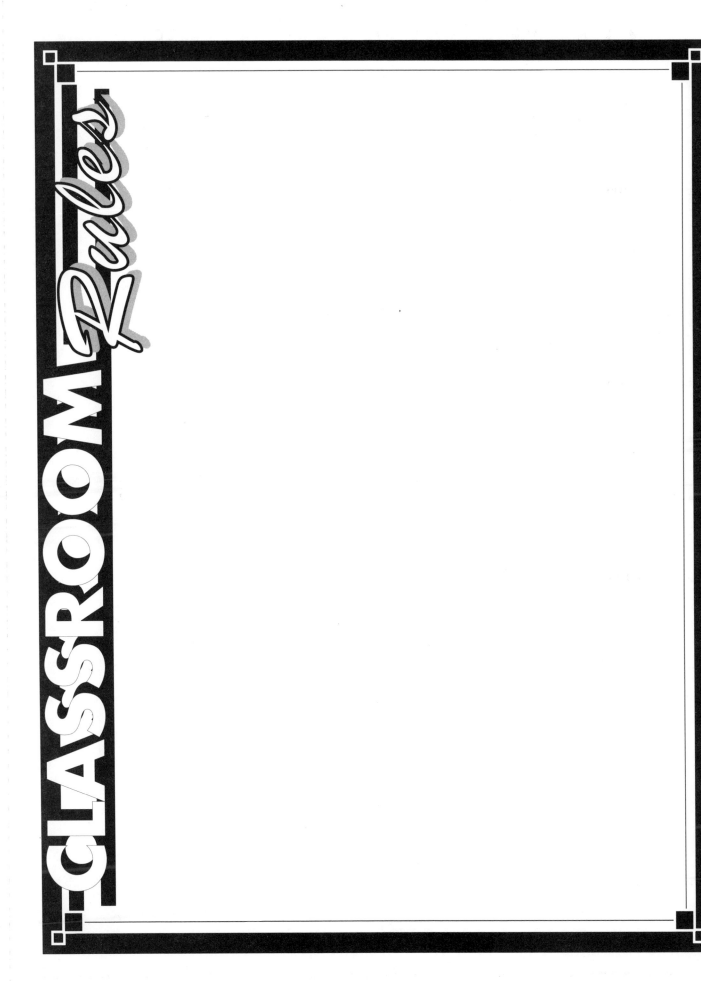

CLASSROOM Rules

Creating Your Classroom Discipline Plan
Positive Recognition

Your general classroom rules are the first part of your classroom discipline plan. The second part of your discipline plan, positive recognition, will help you motivate your students to follow these rules.

Positive recognition is the sincere and meaningful attention you give a student for meeting your expectations—for choosing the responsible behavior that will lead to greater success in school, increased self-esteem and a positive attitude toward the possibilities that lie ahead. Positive recognition is your opportunity to reach out to your students with the caring attitude and reassurance that builds solid relationships between teacher and student. Don't fall into the trap of taking students' appropriate behavior for granted. Let them know when you're proud of them!

The business world has long recognized the value of positively recognizing employees' efforts. Managers understand that positive recognition increases workers' self-esteem, increases their motivation for doing well and results in higher productivity and higher company-wide morale. Recognitions such as "Employee of the Month," tangible rewards and meaningful verbal praise are important corporate management techniques.

When consistently used, positive recognition will:

- Encourage your students to behave appropriately.

- Increase your students' self-esteem.

- Dramatically reduce problem behaviors.

- Create a positive classroom climate for you and your students.

- Help you teach appropriate behavior and establish positive relationships with your students.

> *Refer to pages 57-62 of the revised Assertive Discipline text for an in-depth look at the benefits of positive recognition.*

With these benefits in mind, let's take a look now at five ways you can provide positive recognition to individual students:

1. Praise
2. Positive notes and phone calls home
3. Special privileges
4. Certificates and awards
5. Tangible rewards

Praise

The most meaningful *and* effective means of positive recognition you can give to secondary students are your own words of praise. Complimentary words from a caring teacher can positively effect a student long after the class ends and the student moves on.

It only takes a few seconds to say something positive about a student's responsible behavior or academic achievement. And yet this recognition says a great deal to a student:

> "I care about you. I've noticed your good efforts. I like you, and I'm proud of you."

These are self-esteem-boosting messages that secondary school students need to hear as often as possible.

Praise, then, should be your #1 choice in positive recognition.

To ensure that the praise you give your students is as effective as possible, keep these guidelines in mind:

• Effective praise is personal.

High school, with its fast-paced schedules, bells and busy hallways, can seem like a pretty impersonal place—for freshmen and new students as well as third- or fourth-year veterans. Let students know that they are more than nameless faces in the crowd. Maximize the impact of praise by including the student's name in your comments. Personal praise will open the door to making a vital connection with each and every student.

> "Juan, that was a great question you raised in class today. It made the discussion a lot more interesting for everyone."

• Effective praise must be genuine.

Teenagers recognize sincere words when they hear them. Make sure your words of praise genuinely reflect your own feelings of pride in a student's accomplishments. If your words ring false they won't mean a thing.

• Effective praise is descriptive and specific.

Praise will be most effective when it refers to something specific the student has accomplished. A specific comment such as, "I've noticed how well prepared for class you've been all this week, Amanda, and your efforts are paying off in better grades!" sounds much more meaningful than, "Great job, Amanda."

Secondary teachers often avoid positive reinforcement (particularly praise) because they feel that high school students simply cannot handle it. Some are reluctant to give praise because students, uncomfortable with the recognition, may immediately revert to the negative behavior they *are* comfortable with. Others feel their praise is not valued because the student simply shrugs it off, ignores it or makes a face that suggests extreme discomfort!

We thus are presented with a paradox: Adolescents are among the neediest of all age children for praise, support and validation. Yet they make it the hardest for the adults in their lives to give it to them. The need to be cool, the need for peer acceptance, and the struggle to separate from parents and school often make them overtly resistant to any attempt to positively reinforce.

But in spite of the impression they give, secondary students do appreciate and want positive recognition. Your challenge as a teacher is to provide it with skill and care. It is up to you, therefore, to exercise professional judgment and sensitivity when praising a student. Some students will appreciate and enjoy a verbal and public "round of applause" from time to time. Other students will require a very private word of praise from you. Your goal is to build a student's self-esteem. With that in mind, deliver your praise in a manner that will be best received by the individual student.

Additional techniques contained in Section One will help you develop a selection of positive recognition ideas that will allow you to effectively reach and motivate most of your students. Applied with sensitivity and skill, these techniques will help you overcome students' roadblocks to acceptance of praise and validation.

It's Your Turn

Start thinking now about all of the opportunities you have each day to recognize your students' successes—all of the moments when an admiring word from you can make a big difference in a student's life. Jot notes in your plan book reminding yourself to look for students' positive behavior (or other achievement), then say something about it! Some teachers set a goal to give a minimum of five compliments per class period. Make that your goal, too, and you will be sure to positively reach at least 25-30 students each day.

Timely Reminders

As an extra reminder to praise students, make a copy of the "Time for Smart Choices" poster on page 15. Hang this reminder on the classroom wall right next to the clock. Throughout the day as you glance at the clock, this poster will be a reminder to keep looking for positive behavior —smart behavior choices— to reinforce.

Looking for just the right moment to say "good for you?"

It is so easy to fall into the trap of being negative, yet there are hundreds of opportunities to praise students each day. Don't let these moments slip by. To help you further develop the praise habit, we've put together a list of "50 Opportunities to say 'You're Terrific'" (page 16). Keep this sheet in your desk or plan book and review it from time to time as a reminder of all the occasions throughout the school day in which you can verbally recognize a student's good behavior.

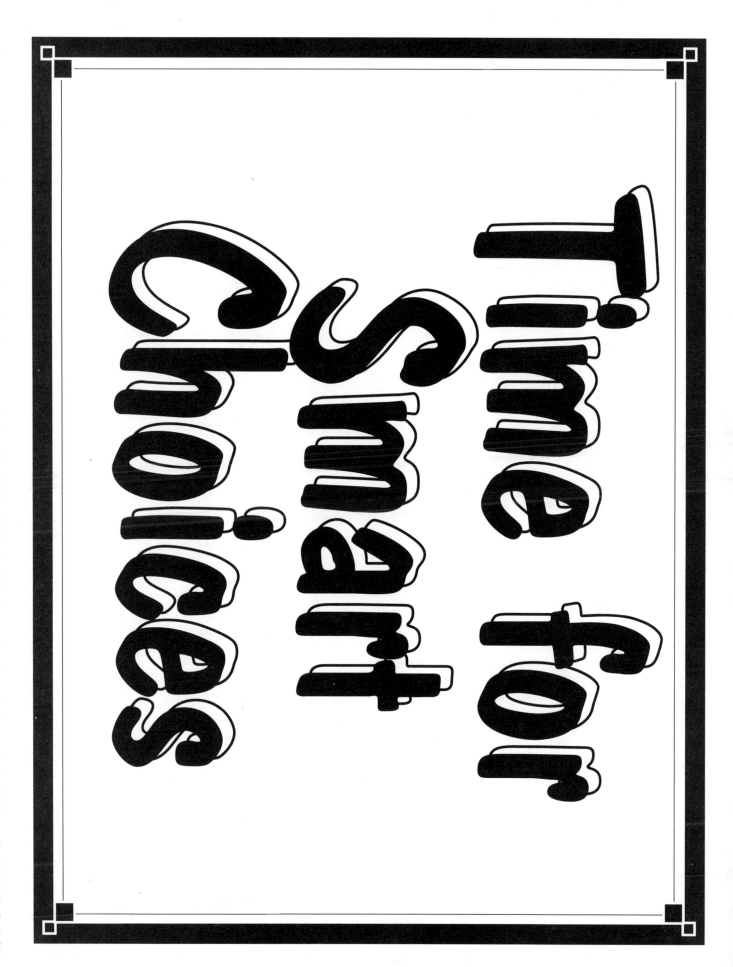

Time for Smart Choices

50 OPPORTUNITIES TO SAY "YOU'RE TERRIFIC"

Praise students for:

1 entering the classroom quietly

2 arriving to class on time

3 cooperating while teacher takes attendance

4 returning school forms on time

5 transitioning into an activity

6 following directions

7 saying "please" and "thank you"

8 listening attentively

9 helping a classmate

10 bringing necessary materials to class

11 handing in homework

12 being a polite audience at an assembly

13 beginning work right away

14 asking questions when unsure

15 good behavior during a test

16 participating in a class discussion

17 walking appropriately in the halls

18 working cooperatively with a partner

19 a performance in a play or presentation

20 putting away supplies and equipment

21 good effort on an assignment

22 assisting a new student

23 sharing school experiences with parents

24 making up missed assignments

25 making a new friend

26 good effort on a long-term project

27 sharing

28 being sensitive to others' feelings

29 learning a new skill

30 appropriate use of school property

31 returning borrowed books and materials

32 showing enthusiasm

33 being responsible for a classroom job

34 offering help without being asked

35 not wasting paper and supplies

36 staying on task

37 telling the truth

38 accepting a new challenge

39 behaving when a guest is in the room

40 reading at home

41 participating in school functions

42 demonstrating a positive attitude

43 giving one's best effort

44 participating in a community improvement project

45 participating in a group activity

46 remaining calm during a problem situation

47 showing creativity

48 keeping busy when work is finished

49 taking turns

50 working cooperatively with an aide or volunteer

Positive Notes and Phone Calls to Parents

Usually parents are only notified when there is a problem with their child at school. But how often do parents of secondary students hear *positive* news from teachers?

Don't underestimate the impact of positive communication between school and home! No matter how independent or aloof your students may appear, they still need encouragement and support during their high school years. The goal of a positive note or phone call is to share with parents "good news" about their child. It is important for adolescents to know that you think enough of their success to share it with their parents.

It's also a great way to establish positive relationships with parents. Should a problem arise during the year, it will be much easier to gain parental support if you have already begun building a positive foundation.

Finally, parents have enough to worry about when it comes to teenage sons and daughters. They will welcome and appreciate your encouraging comments about their child—comments that may be the first positive words they've heard about the child in years.

Positive phone calls and notes don't take much time, but they pay big dividends and need to become a regular part of your planning for positive recognition.

Here's what a positive phone call to a parent might sound like.

"Mr. Gibson? This is Mrs. Gray, Todd's biology teacher. I just wanted to take a moment to let you to know that Todd has made a terrific start in my class this year. We've spent a lot of time this first week going over lab procedures, and talking about the course. Todd has been enthusiastic in class, and comes prepared every day. It looks like he's in for a terrific year.

"Please tell Todd that I called and let him know how pleased I am to have him in my class."

Just that easy and just that quick. In a few brief moments this teacher has established a positive relationship with a parent and boosted the self-esteem of a student.

And here's what a positive note might say:

> Dear Mr. and Mrs. Arias,
>
> Just a note to let you know what a great start Nicole is making in my English class. I can tell by the work she's turning in that she's working hard on her writing assignments. She has a real flair for expressing herself.
>
> Sincerely,

It's Your Turn

Once you recognize how easy it really is to make positive contact with parents, you'll be convinced that it's an effective use of your time. The suggestions that follow will help you develop this positive parent involvement habit.

First, set goals!

If you're concerned that you have too many students to make positive parent communication a viable option, look at it this way: Set a goal to make a specific number of positive phone calls each week and to send a specific number of positive notes home each week. Just two contacts a day (10 a week) will guarantee that you reach 40 parents a month with good news. To make sure that all students receive this important attention, keep track of your positive contacts on the Positive Parent Communication Log on page 19. Create a sheet for each class, and check off whenever good news goes home.

Once you break the ice with parents, particularly with good news, you may find yourself picking up the phone more often—just to pass along some friendly, encouraging words.

Next, remember the good things that happen!

It's not always easy to remember the positive things students do during a busy day—especially when you have many students coming in and out of your classes. The answer? Use the Positive Memos on page 20 to jot down positive comments you want to remember and later share with parents in a phone call or in a note. Run off copies of the memos and keep them close at hand—different colors for different classes. During the day if something "memo"rable happens that you'd like to communicate, write it down! In some cases you may wish to keep this memo as part of a student's documentation file.

Finally, be sure to share the good news!

Use the reproducible notes on pages 21-24 any time you want to share your pride in a student's achievement. The "subject specific" artwork on each note will let a parent know immediately who the note is from. Run off copies of these notes, keep them handy, and use them frequently! (Keep track of notes sent home on the Positive Parent Communication Log.)

Fold-a-Note Cards

This is a perfect—and easy—way to send a message. Reproduce, cut along the dotted line and you've got two note cards ready to use. Just write, staple shut, address and mail.

At the beginning of the year, take a few minutes to have each student address at least one note. Collect and keep ready to use.

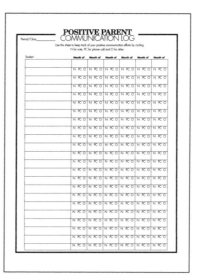

POSITIVE PARENT
COMMUNICATION LOG

Period/Class_____

Use this sheet to keep track of your positive communication efforts by circling
N for note, PC for phone call and O for other.

Student	Month of	Month of	Month of	Month of	Month of	Month of
	N PC O	N PC O	N PC O	N PC O	N PC O	N PC O
	N PC O	N PC O	N PC O	N PC O	N PC O	N PC O
	N PC O	N PC O	N PC O	N PC O	N PC O	N PC O
	N PC O	N PC O	N PC O	N PC O	N PC O	N PC O
	N PC O	N PC O	N PC O	N PC O	N PC O	N PC O
	N PC O	N PC O	N PC O	N PC O	N PC O	N PC O
	N PC O	N PC O	N PC O	N PC O	N PC O	N PC O
	N PC O	N PC O	N PC O	N PC O	N PC O	N PC O
	N PC O	N PC O	N PC O	N PC O	N PC O	N PC O
	N PC O	N PC O	N PC O	N PC O	N PC O	N PC O
	N PC O	N PC O	N PC O	N PC O	N PC O	N PC O
	N PC O	N PC O	N PC O	N PC O	N PC O	N PC O
	N PC O	N PC O	N PC O	N PC O	N PC O	N PC O
	N PC O	N PC O	N PC O	N PC O	N PC O	N PC O
	N PC O	N PC O	N PC O	N PC O	N PC O	N PC O
	N PC O	N PC O	N PC O	N PC O	N PC O	N PC O
	N PC O	N PC O	N PC O	N PC O	N PC O	N PC O
	N PC O	N PC O	N PC O	N PC O	N PC O	N PC O
	N PC O	N PC O	N PC O	N PC O	N PC O	N PC O
	N PC O	N PC O	N PC O	N PC O	N PC O	N PC O
	N PC O	N PC O	N PC O	N PC O	N PC O	N PC O
	N PC O	N PC O	N PC O	N PC O	N PC O	N PC O

POSITIVE MEMO

Student's name_____ Parent's name_____

Phone number_____ Date_____ Period/Class_____

Positive news to share with parents:

_____

_____

_____

_____

_____

POSITIVE MEMO

Student's name_____ Parent's name_____

Phone number_____ Date_____ Period/Class_____

Positive news to share with parents:

_____

_____

_____

_____

_____

POSITIVE MEMO

Student's name_____ Parent's name_____

Phone number_____ Date_____ Period/Class_____

Positive news to share with parents:

_____

_____

_____

_____

_____

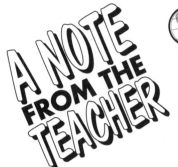

_____
Subject   Period

_____
Subject   Period

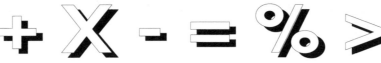

_____
Subject   Period

_____
Subject   Period

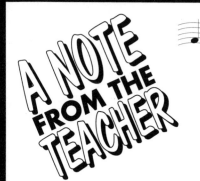

_____
Subject   Period

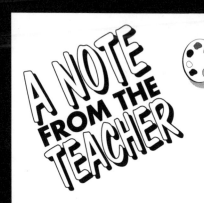

_____
Subject   Period

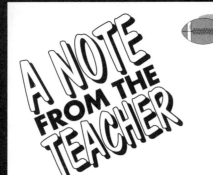

_____
Subject   Period

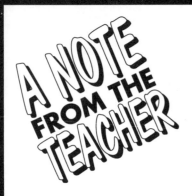

_____
Subject   Period

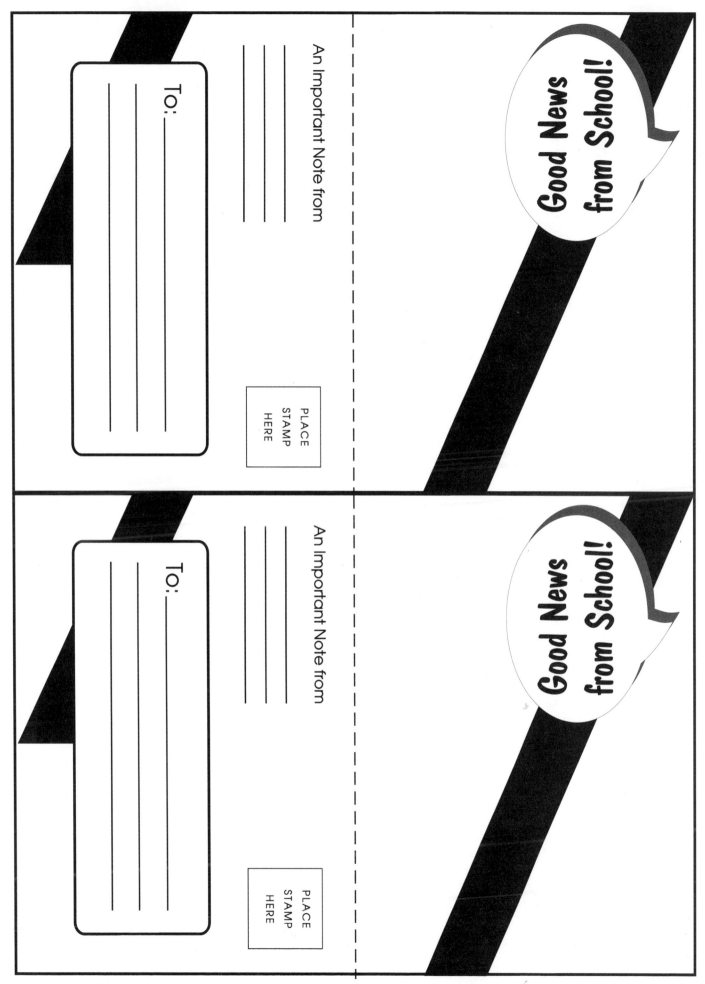

Behavior Awards and Notes

Recognition for a job well done is appreciated by students of any age. Secondary students, no matter how "cool" they appear to be, are no different than any of us when we are presented with tangible evidence that someone has noticed our good work.

They may stuff the "award" in a book with scarcely a glance, but chances are good that that piece of paper will later be taken out at home, read carefully and perhaps even tucked away among the student's mementos.

The important thing to remember when giving a secondary student a recognition is to take the time to add a personal note. A generic reproducible award with a hastily scrawled signature may not mean much, but a few lines of your own comments will mean a great deal.

Tell students that one way you'll recognize their responsible behavior throughout the year is by giving them special recognitions that let them *and* their parents know what a great job they are doing in school.

It's Your Turn

On the following pages you will find a variety of behavior recognitions designed especially for secondary students.

Quick-Notes to Parents
These quick-notes are an easy way to send a speedy positive message to parents. Keep a stack close by, and when you are grading papers and would like to share some positive news just fill one out and staple to the paper. A great way to stay in touch with parents.

Quick-Notes to Students
A teacher's written comments to a student can have a long-lasting and positive impact. Quick Notes are a simple way to pass along a few good words. Just fill out and staple to returned papers.

Clock Busters

Time is a precious commodity to a fifteen or sixteen-year-old. That's why Clock Busters tickets will be well-worth students' good behavior efforts. A Clock Buster ticket, earned for appropriate behavior, entitles a student to an extra day to turn in an assignment.

Here's how to use Clock Busters tickets:

Explain to students that when they receive a Clock Busters ticket they are to save it to use sometime when they need an extra day to complete an assignment. (Clarify any exceptions you may have, such as the due date for a long-term paper.) When they wish to redeem a ticket, students fill in a description of the assignment, the due date and sign the slip. To make record-keeping easy for you, draw a circle in your record book for the assignment due that day. The next day, the empty circle will remind you that the assignment from the day before has come due.

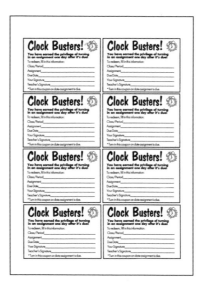

Privilege Passes

Secondary students love getting out of class, even if it's only for a minute or two. Now they can earn the privilege by demonstrating exemplary classroom behavior. Students will gladly give their best efforts to earn the privilege of leaving class to get a drink, or go to the library, school bookstore, or restroom. When you want to reward a student, just fill in his or her name on a Privilege Pass and "pass" along a well-deserved award.

Good Behavior Bookmark/Raffle Ticket Combos

There's a bonus attached to these bookmarks! Each bookmark also contains a raffle ticket. Each time a student is awarded a bookmark, he or she also earns the right to enter a raffle drawing. The student fills the ticket out and deposits it into a class collection box. Once a week (or every two weeks, etc.) the teacher draws a pre-determined number of tickets and awards privileges or prizes.

Or try this: At the beginning of the week, pass out a bookmark to each student. Explain that as the week goes by you will recognize responsible behavior by allowing students to enter their ticket portion in a class raffle.

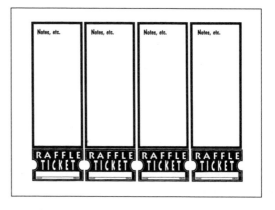

"Notables"

Just for students—these open-ended positive notes (pages 34-35) are designed to provide you with an appealing graphic background that will enhance your message and help you communicate your sincere words of appreciation.

Get the Community Involved!

Free items from local merchants are great positive rewards and motivators for students. This idea takes a little work up front, but the results are worth it, both in terms of motivating students *and* in generating community involvement.

Here's what to do:

1. Make a copies of the School-Community Positive Recognition cards on page 36.

2. Notice that the card ends contain space for a student's name, name of school and teacher's signature. The remaining spaces are blank.

3. Contact local merchants, asking them to be a part of a positive recognition program for your classes. Explain that you want to give meaningful recognition to students who are making responsible behavior choices—and that as a member of the community the recognition they can offer is important.

Ask each merchant to offer a "freebie" that the student receives when he or she brings a signed School Community Positive Recognition Card into the place of business. Explain that students who are in possession of these cards will be those who have earned them through responsible behavior. (After a prize is redeemed, the merchant can "x" out the box or punch a hole through it.)

Here are some examples of recognitions that merchants typically offer:

Movie theater:	Free box of popcorn
Fast food restaurant:	Free hamburger
Convenience store:	Free soda or frozen "slushy" drink
Skating rink	Free pass or free skate rental
Bowling alley	Free game or free shoe rental
Video store	Free video rental
Frozen yogurt	Free serving

4. Once you have collected enough recognitions, list them in the spaces on the card. Duplicate, cut out and keep available for use. Decide on parameters for use of the card (how a student can earn one) and introduce to students.

5. Stay in contact with contributing merchants, and let them know how much you appreciate their involvement. Encourage students to say thanks, too.

QUICK NOTE
to Parents

To:_____

Just a note to let you know that

_____

_____

_____

_____

_____

_____
Signed   Date

QUICK NOTE
to Parents

To:_____

Just a note to let you know that

_____

_____

_____

_____

_____

_____
Signed   Date

QUICK NOTE
to Parents

To:_____

Just a note to let you know that

_____

_____

_____

_____

_____

_____
Signed   Date

QUICK NOTE
to Parents

To:_____

Just a note to let you know that

_____

_____

_____

_____

_____

_____
Signed   Date

QUICK NOTE

to Students

To:_____

Just a note to
let you know that _____

_____

_____

_____

_____

_____

Signed   Date

QUICK NOTE

to Students

To:_____

Just a note to
let you know that _____

_____

_____

_____

_____

_____

Signed   Date

QUICK NOTE

to Students

To:_____

Just a note to
let you know that _____

_____

_____

_____

_____

_____

Signed   Date

QUICK NOTE

to Students

To:_____

Just a note to
let you know that _____

_____

_____

_____

_____

_____

Signed   Date

Clock Busters!

You have earned the privilege of turning in an assignment one day after it's due!

To redeem, fill in this information:

Class/Period_____

Assignment_____

Due Date_____

Your Signature_____

Teacher's Signature_____

*Turn in this coupon on date assignment is due.

Clock Busters!

You have earned the privilege of turning in an assignment one day after it's due!

To redeem, fill in this information:

Class/Period_____

Assignment_____

Due Date_____

Your Signature_____

Teacher's Signature_____

*Turn in this coupon on date assignment is due.

Clock Busters!

You have earned the privilege of turning in an assignment one day after it's due!

To redeem, fill in this information:

Class/Period_____

Assignment_____

Due Date_____

Your Signature_____

Teacher's Signature_____

*Turn in this coupon on date assignment is due.

Clock Busters!

You have earned the privilege of turning in an assignment one day after it's due!

To redeem, fill in this information:

Class/Period_____

Assignment_____

Due Date_____

Your Signature_____

Teacher's Signature_____

*Turn in this coupon on date assignment is due.

Clock Busters!

You have earned the privilege of turning in an assignment one day after it's due!

To redeem, fill in this information:

Class/Period_____

Assignment_____

Due Date_____

Your Signature_____

Teacher's Signature_____

*Turn in this coupon on date assignment is due.

Clock Busters!

You have earned the privilege of turning in an assignment one day after it's due!

To redeem, fill in this information:

Class/Period_____

Assignment_____

Due Date_____

Your Signature_____

Teacher's Signature_____

*Turn in this coupon on date assignment is due.

Clock Busters!

You have earned the privilege of turning in an assignment one day after it's due!

To redeem, fill in this information:

Class/Period_____

Assignment_____

Due Date_____

Your Signature_____

Teacher's Signature_____

*Turn in this coupon on date assignment is due.

Clock Busters!

You have earned the privilege of turning in an assignment one day after it's due!

To redeem, fill in this information:

Class/Period_____

Assignment_____

Due Date_____

Your Signature_____

Teacher's Signature_____

*Turn in this coupon on date assignment is due.

privilege PASS

Student Signature
_____
Teacher Signature

privilege PASS

Student Signature
_____
Teacher Signature

privilege PASS

Student Signature
_____
Teacher Signature

privilege PASS

Student Signature
_____
Teacher Signature

privilege PASS

Student Signature
_____
Teacher Signature

privilege PASS

Student Signature
_____
Teacher Signature

privilege PASS

Student Signature
_____
Teacher Signature

privilege PASS

Student Signature
_____
Teacher Signature

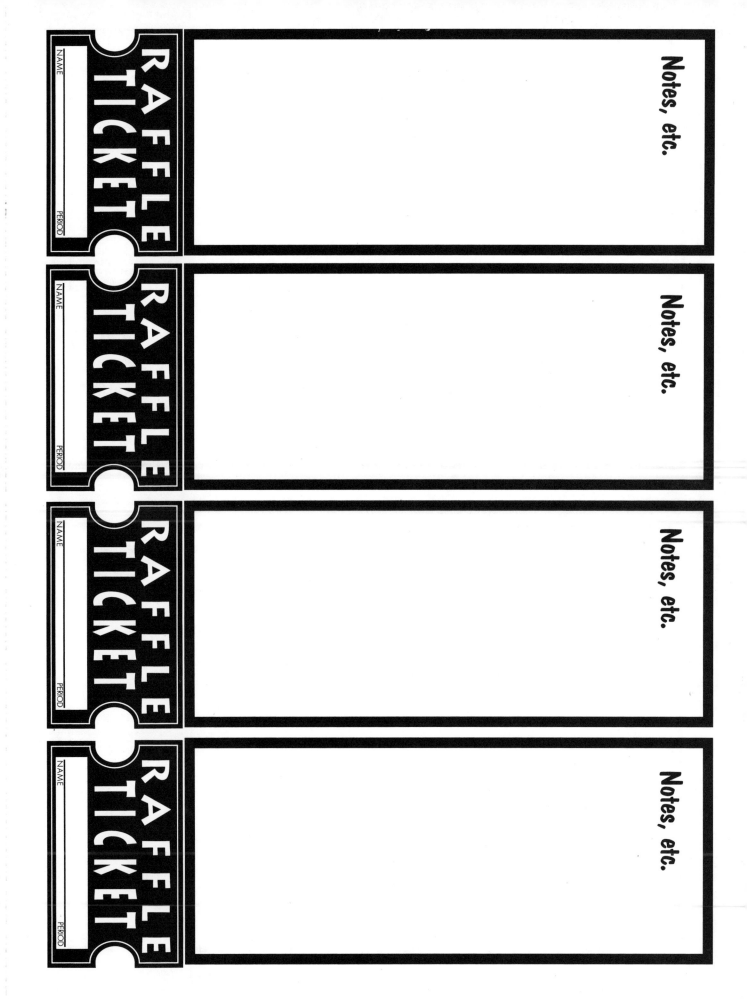

RAFFLE TICKET

NAME

PERIOD

Notes, etc.

RAFFLE TICKET

NAME

PERIOD

Notes, etc.

RAFFLE TICKET

NAME

PERIOD

Notes, etc.

RAFFLE TICKET

NAME

PERIOD

Notes, etc.

A MESSAGE
FROM THE
TEACHER

School-Community Positive Recognition

Student's name

School

Teacher's signature

School-Community Positive Recognition

Student's name

School

Teacher's signature

School-Community Positive Recognition

Student's name

School

Teacher's signature

School-Community Positive Recognition

Student's name

School

Teacher's signature

Special Privileges

When you want to recognize a student's positive behavior, and motivate him or her to continue that behavior, allow the student to take part in an activity that he or she particularly enjoys.

Special privileges are great motivators because students like to receive them and they don't have to cost anything to give.

Here are some ideas to get you started. Add ideas of your own that will appeal to your students on the lines that follow.

- First excused after class
- Choose any seat in class for a day, a week, etc.
- Listen to music on cassette with headset
- 10 minutes free time
- Extra computer time
- Work on favorite activity
- May leave room to get a drink

- _____
- _____
- _____
- _____
- _____
- _____
- _____
- _____
- _____
- _____
- _____
- _____
- _____
- _____
- _____

It's Your Turn

Just ask 'em!

Not sure what special privileges will motivate your students? Your students will be more than happy to give their opinions on this matter! Give students the "Wish List" menu on the next page. Before you reproduce the list, write some privileges that you would be comfortable offering to your students. After distributing, ask students to write in appropriate suggestions of their own.

Tell students that you want their feedback because throughout the year you will be awarding special privileges to students who exhibit responsible behavior at school. Tie this activity into a brief class discussion and you're sure to gather lots of motivating suggestions!

You Earned It!

When a student earns a special privilege for responsible behavior choices, fill out a "You Earned It" coupon. These open-ended coupons are great for communicating positive recognition to students *and* they're easy to complete. Add some praise of your own when you hand out the coupons and make the recognition even more meaningful.

"Phillip, you worked with your lab partner today without any disagreements or problems. Because of that, you completed your experiment on time. Here's a coupon worth an extra 5 points on Friday's quiz. You earned it!"

Get parents involved, too!

Send home a small supply of "You Earned It" coupons to parents. In a brief note, encourage them to use the coupons at home to congratulate their children for good schoolwork, responsible behavior at school or at home, or as a recognition for being a caring member of the family. (Back-to-School Night is a good time to explain these coupons to parents and distribute copies to parents.)

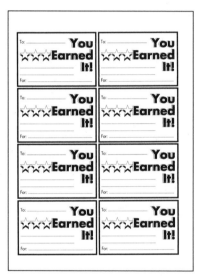

WISH LIST OF SPECIAL PRIVILEGES

Name_____ Class/Period_____

Check off three things that you like to do best in class. If you have any
suggestions of your own, add them to the list.

☐ _____   ☐ _____
☐ _____   ☐ _____
☐ _____   ☐ _____
☐ _____   ☐ _____
☐ _____   ☐ _____

WISH LIST OF SPECIAL PRIVILEGES

Name_____ Class/Period_____

Check off three things that you like to do best in class. If you have any
suggestions of your own, add them to the list.

☐ _____   ☐ _____
☐ _____   ☐ _____
☐ _____   ☐ _____
☐ _____   ☐ _____
☐ _____   ☐ _____

WISH LIST OF SPECIAL PRIVILEGES

Name_____ Class/Period_____

Check off three things that you like to do best in class. If you have any
suggestions of your own, add them to the list.

☐ _____   ☐ _____
☐ _____   ☐ _____
☐ _____   ☐ _____
☐ _____   ☐ _____
☐ _____   ☐ _____

To: _____

★★★ **You Earned It!**

_____

For: _____

To: _____

★★★ **You Earned It!**

_____

For: _____

To: _____

★★★ **You Earned It!**

_____

For: _____

To: _____

★★★ **You Earned It!**

_____

For: _____

To: _____

★★★ **You Earned It!**

_____

For: _____

To: _____

★★★ **You Earned It!**

_____

For: _____

To: _____

★★★ **You Earned It!**

_____

For: _____

To: _____

★★★ **You Earned It!**

_____

For: _____

Tangible Rewards

Most secondary students are motivated by praise, positive notes and special privileges. You may, however, have one or two students who simply do not respond to these positive reinforcers. There are times when tangible rewards such as a small prize or other token are the only positives that will work—the only way you can motivate a student. When needed, use tangible rewards, but use them with care.

Follow these guidelines:

- Be sure to give a tangible reward immediately after you have observed the desired behavior. You want the student to associate this behavior with the reward.

- Whenever you give a student a tangible reward, always pair it with your own praise such as,

  "Bill, here's a discount ticket for a cheeseburger and fries. It's yours for sitting quietly and paying attention during the lecture today. I really appreciate your cooperation."

  "Dennine, here are two mints—one for you and one for a friend—my way of saying thanks for taking your seat so quickly and quietly when you came into the classroom today. We were all able to get to work right away."

Tangible rewards are particularly effective on those hard-to-motivate days when students tend to become overly excited (on Fridays, days before holidays, and days when special school events are scheduled).

It's Your Turn

We've looked at five ways you can positively reinforce students for following the rules of the classroom:

1 Praise

2 Positive notes and phone calls home

3 Special privileges

4 Behavior awards

5 Tangible awards

Now it's time to plan the positives you will use with individual students in your own classroom. As you plan, be sure to include positives that you are comfortable giving, that students will enjoy receiving and, most importantly, ones that you will be able to give frequently and consistently.

When you're finished planning, write your positives on the poster on page 42. (Tuck the finished poster away with your supplies. You'll be using it when you introduce your classroom discipline plan to your students.)

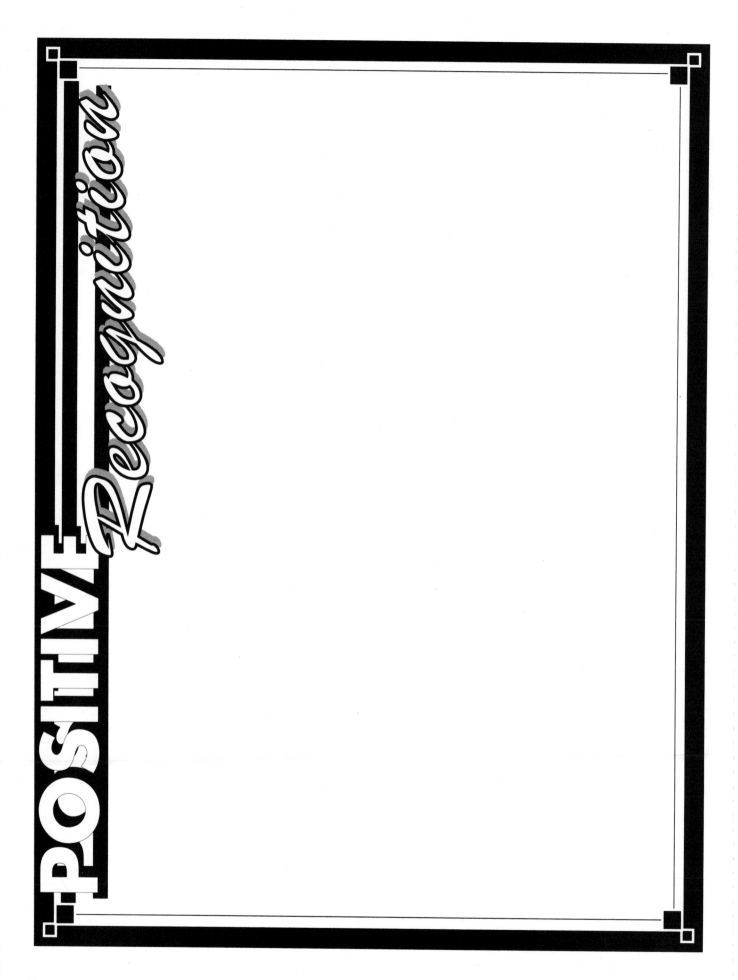

POSITIVE Recognition

Classwide Positive Recognition

Just as you recognize individual students for their appropriate behavior, you can also recognize your entire class for meeting expectations. A classwide positive recognition system is an effective way of motivating students to behave and is easy to use.

What is a classwide positive recognition system?

A classwide positive recognition system is a program in which all of your students, not just one student, work together toward a positive reward that will be given to the entire class.

The goal of a classwide recognition system is to motivate students to learn a new behavior or to work on improving a problem behavior. It shows students the importance of working together in a cooperative manner to achieve a common goal.

Keep these points in mind when considering a classwide recognition system:

- A powerful reason why a classwide recognition system works well with older students is because it makes use of peer pressure. It's not uncommon for students to cooperatively remind each other, "Get in your seat! We only need four more points to get radio time on Friday."

- A classwide recognition system is particularly effective when working on a specific classwide problem behavior such as students noisily entering the classroom.

- A classwide recognition system is also effective at the beginning of the year in classes such as PE, art and science (labs) where students need to learn important procedures (getting and setting up equipment, cleaning up).

- To be effective, a classwide recognition system should be implemented only as needed throughout the year. It is not meant to be in effect at all times. A classwide recognition system is designed to be used as a prescription for correcting a specific problem.

Here's how to set up a classwide recognition program:

1. Pick a system that you are comfortable with and that is appropriate to the age of your students. On pages 44-46 you will find directions and artwork for creating a positive behavior chart especially designed for secondary students.

2. Choose a classwide reward that you are comfortable giving, but make sure that whatever reward the class earns, it is something they will want to work toward.

Here are some ideas for classwide rewards:

- Class game: Bingo, tic-tac-toe, trivial pursuit (These games can be educationally oriented too—serving as a review!)

- Special movie or video

- Invite a special visitor to class

- Popcorn party

- 1/2 hour study hall to get homework done early

- Listen to music in class

- Students bring snacks to share in class

3. Make sure students are able to earn the reward in a timely manner. Set a goal for how quickly you want the class to earn a reward. Then monitor the frequency with which you are awarding points to ensure that you and the students are on track. Secondary students typically should be able to earn the classwide reward in one to two weeks.

4. Once the class has earned points toward a classwide reward, do not take away points for misbehavior. Also, keep in mind that all students, regardless of negative consequences they may have earned individually, must participate in the classwide reward. If you impose a consequence and take away the classwide reward, you are providing two consequences for one misbehavior.

It's Your Turn

The following pages contain artwork and instructions for creating a positive behavior chart for your classroom.

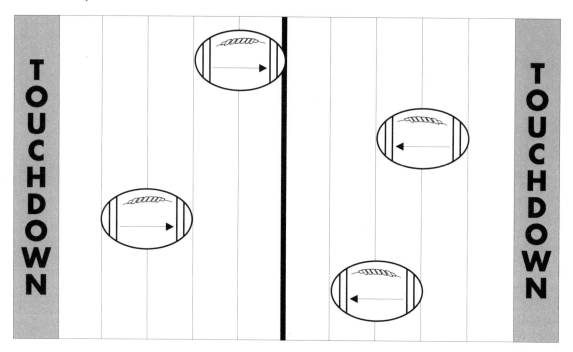

Touchdown!

Here's a classwide recognition system that will boost class spirit and encourage everyone to work together!

1. Cut out a football (pages 45-46) for every class that you want involved in this positive recognition "game."

2. To start, place footballs on the 20-yard line. The object is for each class, represented by a football, to advance forward and arrive at the opposite end zone before any of the other classes.

3. When students in a class meet predetermined behavioral goals, such as entering the classroom quietly or bringing all materials to class, the class earns the right to move forward to the next yard line. The first class to reach the end zone wins.

Note: This classwide recognition system can also be used with an individual class not in competition with another.

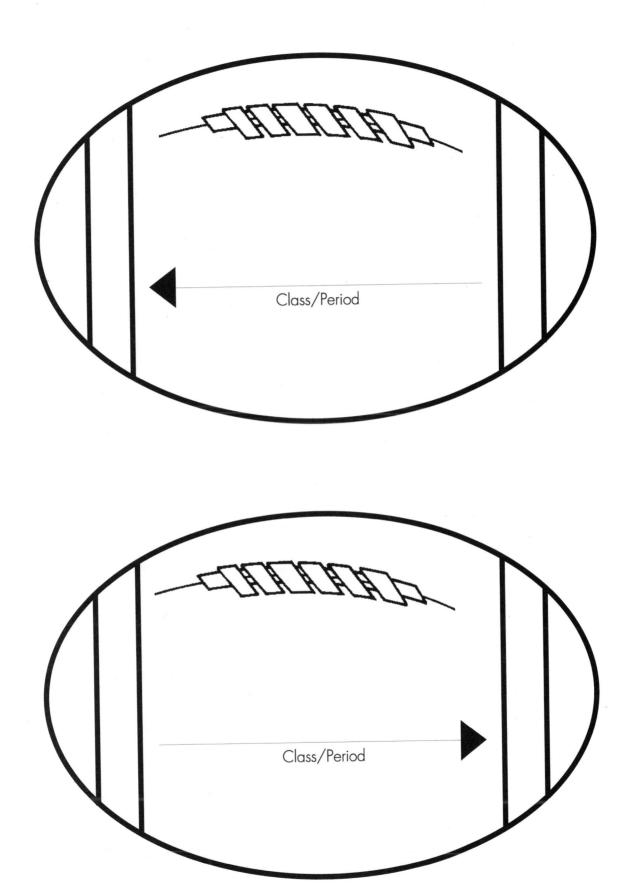

Class/Period

Class/Period

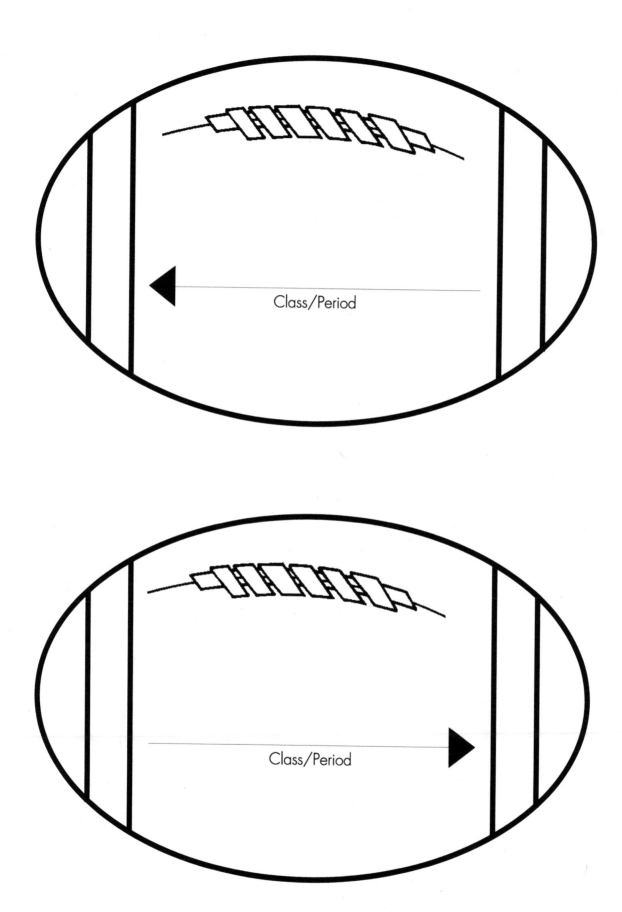

Creating Your Classroom Discipline Plan
Consequences

In spite of the care you take in choosing your rules, and in spite of your consistent attention to positive recognition, there will of course be times when some students will choose not to follow the rules of your classroom. When this disruptive behavior occurs, you must be prepared to deal with it calmly and quickly.

Consequences are the third part of your classroom discipline plan.

Why are consequences important?

By carefully planning consequences, by knowing in advance what you will do when students misbehave, you won't be caught off guard or left wondering how to respond to a student's misbehavior. And that means that students will be treated fairly and *you* will feel less stress.

Follow these guidelines when choosing consequences for your classroom:

• Consequences are a choice.

Students in grades 9 through 12 are realizing that only they are responsible for their actions and their behavior. It's important, therefore, that consequences be presented to students as a choice. When a teacher gives students a choice, he or she places responsibility where it belongs, on the student.

For example:

Teacher: Jordan, the rule is no yelling. If you break a rule again, you will choose to stay one minute after class. It's your choice.

Jordan: Okay. (*Within two minutes, Jordan yells to a friend across the room.*)

Teacher: Jordan, you're yelling again. You've chosen to stay one minute after class.

*Remember—**choice** is the key word.* When you give students a choice, they learn that they can be in control of what happens to them. Keep in mind that consequences are *not* punishment. Consequences are actions students know will occur should they choose to break the rules of the classroom. Consequences must be seen as natural outcomes of inappropriate behavior. After all, the point is to stop inappropriate behavior.

• Consequences do not have to be severe to be effective.

Teachers often think that the more severe a consequence, the more impact it will have on a student. This is not true. The key to effective consequences is that they are used *consistently*. It is the inevitability of the consequence, not the severity, that makes it effective. Minimal consequences, such as remaining in the classroom one minute after the dismissal bell can be as effective as after-school detention when they are given consistently.

And keep this in mind: The easier it is for you to give consequences, the more likely it will be that you will use them.

• Consequences must be something that students do not like, but they must never be physically or psychologically harmful.

How to Use Consequences:
Establishing a Discipline Hierarchy

The best way to use consequences with your students is to organize them into a discipline hierarchy as part of your classroom discipline plan.

A discipline hierarchy lists consequences in the order in which they will be imposed for disruptive behavior within a class period.

- The hierarchy is progressive, starting with a warning.

- The consequences then become gradually more substantial for the second, third, fourth, and fifth time that a student chooses to disrupt.

Here's how the discipline hierarchy works:

First Time a Student Disrupts

Always give a warning the first time a student disrupts or breaks a classroom rule.

This is an important first consequence because a warning gives the student an opportunity to choose more appropriate behavior before a more substantial consequence is received.

Second or Third Time a Student Disrupts

The second or third time a student disrupts in the same period, you need to provide a consequence.

These consequences should be easy to implement and not time consuming. Typical consequences for second or third infractions include staying one minute after class, staying two minutes after class, time out and writing in a behavior journal. (See pages 53-54 for further discussion about these consequences.)

Fourth Time a Student Disrupts

Four disruptions during a class period are completely unacceptable. You need to contact parents if a student disrupts a fourth time in a period.

For some students, involving parents will be the only way you will motivate them to behave appropriately. Students need to know that you will be consistent in the enforcement of this consequence. Any time a student reaches the fourth level of the discipline hierarchy parents must be contacted.

Fifth Time a Student Disrupts

Sending a student to the principal, vice principal, counselor or dean should be the last consequence on your discipline hierarchy.

In preparation for implementing this consequence, you must have already met with your administrator and discussed the actions he or she will take when students are sent to the office (see pages 58-59).

Severe Clause

Sometimes you have to act quickly and decisively to stop a student's disruptive behavior. In cases of severe misbehavior, such as fighting, vandalism, defying a teacher or in some way stopping the entire class from functioning, a student would not receive a warning. He or she loses the right to proceed through the hierarchy of consequences. Severe misbehavior calls for an immediate consequence that will remove the student from the classroom.

Here is a sample discipline hierarchy for a secondary classroom:

First time a student breaks a rule:	Warning
Second time:	Stay after class one minute
Third time:	Report back to class during lunch, recess, before or after school and write in behavior journal
Fourth time:	Call parents
Fifth time:	Send to administrator
Severe Clause:	Send to administrator

Keeping Track of Consequences

For your discipline hierarchy to be simple to use and easy to integrate into your teaching routine—to guarantee the consistency that is key to its effectiveness—you will need a system to keep track of student misbehavior and consequences accrued. You'll need to know at a glance the names of students who have received consequences, and where they are on the hierarchy.

Keeping track doesn't have to be time consuming and, most important, it doesn't have to interrupt your teaching.

One method of keeping track of consequences is the Behavior Tracking Sheet (page 51). Another is the "8 in 1" sheet (page 52).

Using a Behavior Tracking Sheet

Here's how the Behavior Tracking Sheet works:

Make copies of the Behavior Tracking Sheet on page 51. (Designate a different sheet for each class.) Attach to a clipboard and keep close by throughout the day.

Follow these guidelines:

First time a student breaks a rule

Write down his or her name on the sheet and say, for example, "Danny, the rule is 'No yelling.' This is a warning."

- Circle the "Warning" designation on the tracking sheet.

Second time a student breaks a rule

Speak quietly and calmly to the student saying, for example, "Danny, this is the second time you have broken a rule in this classroom today. You have chosen to stay in class one minute after the bell rings."

- Circle the "2" on the tracking sheet, indicating that this is the second infraction of the day. As noted above, the student has been informed that he is to stay in the classroom for one minute after the bell rings.

Third, fourth or fifth time a student breaks a rule.

If a student breaks a rule a third, fourth or fifth time during the period, you must continue speaking quietly and calmly to the student, and continue recording the infractions on the tracking sheet. Make sure that the consequences are given according to your hierarchy. If your third consequence is detention, be sure you follow through. If your fourth consequence is "call parents," be sure that you make that phone call. The success of your discipline plan depends upon your consistency.

Note: For some students you may wish to jot down the rule broken. Then, if you notice a pattern of behavior developing, you will have documentation to help you solve that problem.

BEHAVIOR TRACKING SHEET

WEEK OF _____

Name	MONDAY	TUESDAY	WEDNESDAY	THURSDAY	FRIDAY
Danny R	(Warning) (2) 3 4 5	Warning 2 3 4 5	Warning 2 3 4 5	Warning 2 3 4 5	Warning 2 3 4 5
	Warning 2 3 4 5	Warning 2 3 4 5	Warning 2 3 4 5	Warning 2 3 4 5	Warning 2 3 4 5
	Warning 2 3 4 5	Warning 2 3 4 5	Warning 2 3 4 5	Warning 2 3 4 5	Warning 2 3 4 5
	Warning 2 3 4 5	Warning 2 3 4 5	Warning 2 3 4 5	Warning 2 3 4 5	Warning 2 3 4 5
	Warning 2 3 4 5	Warning 2 3 4 5	Warning 2 3 4 5	Warning 2 3 4 5	Warning 2 3 4 5
	Warning 2 3 4 5	Warning 2 3 4 5	Warning 2 3 4 5	Warning 2 3 4 5	Warning 2 3 4 5
	Warning 2 3 4 5	Warning 2 3 4 5	Warning 2 3 4 5	Warning 2 3 4 5	Warning 2 3 4 5
	Warning 2 3 4 5	Warning 2 3 4 5	Warning 2 3 4 5	Warning 2 3 4 5	Warning 2 3 4 5
	Warning 2 3 4 5	Warning 2 3 4 5	Warning 2 3 4 5	Warning 2 3 4 5	Warning 2 3 4 5
	Warning 2 3 4 5	Warning 2 3 4 5	Warning 2 3 4 5	Warning 2 3 4 5	Warning 2 3 4 5
	Warning 2 3 4 5	Warning 2 3 4 5	Warning 2 3 4 5	Warning 2 3 4 5	Warning 2 3 4 5
	Warning 2 3 4 5	Warning 2 3 4 5	Warning 2 3 4 5	Warning 2 3 4 5	Warning 2 3 4 5
	Warning 2 3 4 5	Warning 2 3 4 5	Warning 2 3 4 5	Warning 2 3 4 5	Warning 2 3 4 5
	Warning 2 3 4 5	Warning 2 3 4 5	Warning 2 3 4 5	Warning 2 3 4 5	Warning 2 3 4 5
	Warning 2 3 4 5	Warning 2 3 4 5	Warning 2 3 4 5	Warning 2 3 4 5	Warning 2 3 4 5
	Warning 2 3 4 5	Warning 2 3 4 5	Warning 2 3 4 5	Warning 2 3 4 5	Warning 2 3 4 5

To the teacher: When a student receives a warning, write the student's name on this tracking sheet. If a student breaks additional rules during that school day, circle each consequence on the appropriate box. For example, if a student receives a warning and chooses not to follow the rules again during the day, you would record   (Warning) (2)(3) 4 5.

BEHAVIOR TRACKING SHEET

WEEK OF _____

Name	MONDAY	TUESDAY	WEDNESDAY	THURSDAY	FRIDAY
	Warning 2 3 4 5	Warning 2 3 4 5	Warning 2 3 4 5	Warning 2 3 4 5	Warning 2 3 4 5
	Warning 2 3 4 5	Warning 2 3 4 5	Warning 2 3 4 5	Warning 2 3 4 5	Warning 2 3 4 5
	Warning 2 3 4 5	Warning 2 3 4 5	Warning 2 3 4 5	Warning 2 3 4 5	Warning 2 3 4 5
	Warning 2 3 4 5	Warning 2 3 4 5	Warning 2 3 4 5	Warning 2 3 4 5	Warning 2 3 4 5
	Warning 2 3 4 5	Warning 2 3 4 5	Warning 2 3 4 5	Warning 2 3 4 5	Warning 2 3 4 5
	Warning 2 3 4 5	Warning 2 3 4 5	Warning 2 3 4 5	Warning 2 3 4 5	Warning 2 3 4 5
	Warning 2 3 4 5	Warning 2 3 4 5	Warning 2 3 4 5	Warning 2 3 4 5	Warning 2 3 4 5
	Warning 2 3 4 5	Warning 2 3 4 5	Warning 2 3 4 5	Warning 2 3 4 5	Warning 2 3 4 5
	Warning 2 3 4 5	Warning 2 3 4 5	Warning 2 3 4 5	Warning 2 3 4 5	Warning 2 3 4 5
	Warning 2 3 4 5	Warning 2 3 4 5	Warning 2 3 4 5	Warning 2 3 4 5	Warning 2 3 4 5
	Warning 2 3 4 5	Warning 2 3 4 5	Warning 2 3 4 5	Warning 2 3 4 5	Warning 2 3 4 5
	Warning 2 3 4 5	Warning 2 3 4 5	Warning 2 3 4 5	Warning 2 3 4 5	Warning 2 3 4 5
	Warning 2 3 4 5	Warning 2 3 4 5	Warning 2 3 4 5	Warning 2 3 4 5	Warning 2 3 4 5
	Warning 2 3 4 5	Warning 2 3 4 5	Warning 2 3 4 5	Warning 2 3 4 5	Warning 2 3 4 5
	Warning 2 3 4 5	Warning 2 3 4 5	Warning 2 3 4 5	Warning 2 3 4 5	Warning 2 3 4 5

To the teacher: When a student receives a warning, write the student's name on this tracking sheet. If a student breaks additional rules during that school day, circle each consequence on the appropriate box. For example, if a student receives a warning and chooses not to follow the rules again during the day, you would record (Warning) ②③ 4 5.

Using an "8 in 1" Tracking Sheet

Here's an easy tracking method that fits right in your pocket!

- Fold a sheet of lined paper into quarters as shown.

- Write the date on the top of the sheet.

- In each of the eight sections (front and back) designate a period:

  Period 1, Period 2, Period 3, etc.

- During the period if a student breaks a rule or disrupts, simply write his or her name, following it with the number of the classroom rule broken. (If you use this method, your classroom rules must be numbered: For example, Rule #1—Follow directions.)

In the sample below, you can see that Jeff Z. has broken Rule #1. Later in the period he breaks Rule #3:

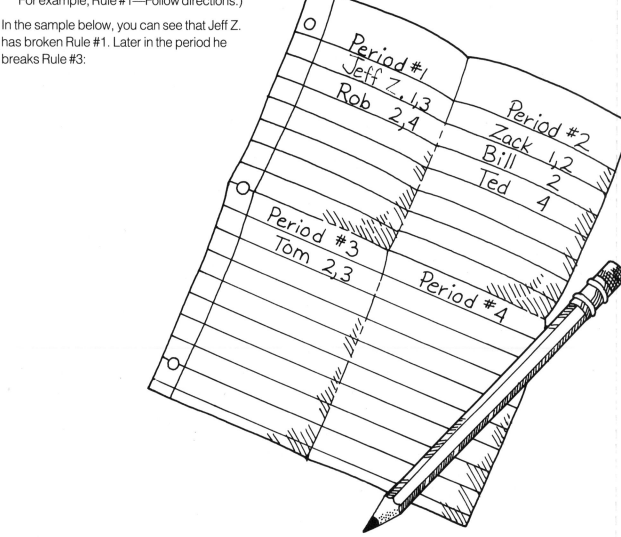

Suggested Consequences

Here are consequences that have proven effective with secondary students:

One-Minute Wait After Class

It sounds deceptively simple, but this is a consequence that students do not like and it works. You simply have the student wait one minute after the other students have been dismissed for recess, lunch, home or the next period. One minute may not seem like a lot of time, but it can be an eternity to a student who wants to be first in line at the cafeteria, sit with a friend on the bus, hurry to his locker or walk to the next class with her group. Don't underestimate the power of this consequence!

A one-minute wait after class is an appropriate consequence for the second time a rule is broken in a period. A two-minute wait is appropriate the third time a rule is broken.

> Note: If use of this consequence (particularly a two-minute wait after class) is likely to cause a student to be late to his or her next class you may wish to discuss this consequence with other staff members. Some teachers resent a colleague keeping a student who is then late to their classes. An alternative to a two-minute wait might be to have the student report back to class during lunch, recess, before or after school to write in a Behavior Journal (see next column).

Time Out—Removing a Student from the Group

Removing a disruptive student from the group is not a new concept, but it can be an effective consequence for some high-school students. Designate a table as the "time-out area," or simply relocate the student to a place in the room where he or she will not be likely to repeat the disruptive behavior. Depending upon the age of the student, a trip to the time-out area could last from five to fifteen minutes.

> Note: It's very important that students not be isolated from the rest of the class for long lengths of time. Keep your time within these limits.

Important! While separated from the rest of the class, the student continues to do his or her classwork.

Written Assignment in Behavior Journal

You want more from consequences than simply stopping a student's disruptive behavior. You also want the student to learn from the experience. That's critical if your students are to learn to choose responsible behavior. You want students to think about their behavior, and how they can choose to behave differently in the future.

When a student breaks a classroom rule, have him or her write a "Behavior Journal" account of this misbehavior either after class, during lunch break, study hall or at home. This written account should include the following points:

1. The rule that was broken.

> *The rule I broke was no swearing.*

2. Why the student chose to break the rule or not follow the direction.

> *I swore at Arnie because he was putting me down. He was making me really mad.*

3. What alternative action the student could have taken that would have been more appropriate.

> *Instead of swearing at Arnie I could have ignored him. I could have walked away and talked to my friends.*

The student signs and dates the Behavior Journal sheet. The sheet should then be added to the student's documentation records. (It can also be sent home to parents as documentation of the student's misbehavior.)

The Behavior Journal sheet can also be used as the focus for a meeting with the student to discuss how teacher and student can work together to improve the problem behavior. Writing in a Behavior Journal helps students accept responsibility for their behavior. It also helps them think about choosing alternative behaviors in the future.

Writing a Letter Home

Here's a consequence that can prove effective with secondary students:

The third time a student breaks a rule he or she writes a brief letter home telling the parent about the rule that was broken. If the student breaks a rule a fourth time, the letter is mailed.

It's Your Turn

On page 55 you will find a reproducible Behavior Journal sheet. Make copies of this sheet and use it as part of your discipline hierarchy. Refer to the guidelines on page 53 for suggestions for use.

Write the consequences you choose on the poster on page 56.

BEHAVIOR JOURNAL

Student's Name _____ Class/Period_____ Date_____

This is the rule I broke: _____

_____

I chose to break this rule because: _____

_____

_____

_____

_____

_____

_____

_____

_____

This is what I could have done instead: _____

_____

_____

_____

_____

_____

_____   _____
Student Signature   Date

CONSEQUENCES

Launching Your Classroom Discipline Plan

Your discipline plan is written. You've chosen the rules for your classroom, the positive recognition you will give when students follow the rules, and the consequences students will receive when they choose to break the rules.

Ready to put it all into action?

Not quite.

The success of your classroom discipline plan depends on more than your planning and involvement alone. It also depends on the informed involvement of others who will be affected by it: your students, your students' parents and your administrator.

In this section of the *Assertive Discipline Secondary Workbook* we will look at techniques for introducing your discipline plan. Also included is a selection of reproducibles to help you plan and carry out an effective introduction.

Talk to Your Administrator About Your Classroom Discipline Plan

No matter how well prepared you are, no matter how consistently and positively you use your discipline plan, you may still have some students that you will not be able to influence on your own. You are going to need the cooperation and assistance of your principal, vice principal, dean or counselor(s). The best way to ensure that cooperation is to involve him or her from the very beginning.

Before you put your classroom discipline plan into effect, you should meet with the appropriate administrator to discuss his or her role in your discipline plan.

This involvement is important for two reasons.

First, if you send a student to the office, according to your discipline hierarchy, your principal (vice principal, dean or counselor) will want to know what steps you have already taken to deal with the problem.

Second, so that you can follow up with a student, you will want to know exactly what action will be taken when a student is sent to the office.

Make an appointment before school begins with the person responsible for dealing with discipline issues at your school. Follow these guidelines for presenting your plan:

Explain your rationale for using a classroom discipline plan.

Explain that you are committed to having a classroom that is safe and orderly, a positive learning environment for your students, and a positive teaching environment for yourself. Explain that this is the reason you have established a classroom discipline plan with rules for behavior, positive recognition for students who choose to follow the rules and consequences for students who choose to break the rules.

Emphasize that you will attempt to handle behavior problems on your own before you ever ask for additional help.

Your principal (vice principal, dean or counselor) needs to know that before you send a student to the office, you will have already taken steps to deal with the student's misbehavior on your own.

Ask for input.

Prepare a copy of your classroom discipline plan for the administrator. During your meeting, ask for input to make sure that he or she is comfortable with all aspects of the plan. If your administrator is not comfortable, ask for assistance in modifying the plan.

Discuss what will happen when a student is sent from your class to the office.

You need to know exactly what will happen when you send a student to the office.

Many administrators follow a hierarchy of consequences, too. Here are some examples:

First time sent to office:

Counsel with the student and suggest other ways the student could have handled the situation.

Second time sent to office:

Hold a parent conference to discuss the problem. Ask parents to support the school's efforts by taking away privileges at home.

Third time sent to office:

In-school suspension. The student does schoolwork outside of the regular classroom and in a closely supervised environment.

Severe:

Counsel with the student and have a parent conference.

It is important that your administrator lets you know what type of disciplinary action will be taken so you can follow up appropriately with parents and student. This follow up can be accomplished by sending a note home or having a short meeting after school.

Discuss what will happen if the administrator is out of the building.

There may be times when you need to remove a disruptive student from your classroom and the principal or vice principal is not in the building. Clarify what you should do in this circumstance.

Here are two alternatives:

- Send student to an alternative person.

- Send student to "time out" in another classroom.

With the prior consent of another teacher, a disruptive student is sent to an higher-grade classroom. When the student reaches the other classroom, he or she sits in a prearranged area away from the rest of the class. The student does not participate in the class activities and either sits quietly or does her own academic work.

Your administrator is an important part of your behavior management team. As such, he or she needs to be informed in advance of the involvement and support you expect. By introducing your discipline plan, you will assure your administrator that you are prepared to deal with student misbehavior on your own before asking for assistance. And by mutually establishing what action your administrator will take, you will help ensure that discipline problems will be handled in a fair and consistent manner by both of you.

Teach Your Classroom Discipline Plan to Your Students

A list of rules posted on your classroom wall is not enough to motivate students to always follow those rules. You must actively involve your students in the plan.

Teaching your classroom discipline plan to your students is as important as any lesson you will teach during the year. This lesson should take place the first day of school—and it must take place in every class that you teach.

The lesson should cover the following points:

1. Explain why you need rules.

2. Teach the rules.

3. Check for understanding.

4. Explain why you have consequences.

5. Teach the consequences.

6. Explain how you will reinforce students who follow the rules.

7. Check for understanding.

Here are some suggestions for teaching your lesson.

1 Discuss the need for rules.

Give a brief rationale for why you have rules in the classroom. Explain that you need to be able to teach, and students need to be able to learn. For both of these things to happen, everyone needs appropriate behavior in the classroom. Make a brief analogy to "on the job" rules, or traffic rules, that students have probably experienced by now. Point out that there are rules in the workplace so that the job can get done. There are traffic rules we must obey so people can safely get from one place to another. Likewise, there are classroom rules so that students can get their job done at school—safely and successfully.

2 Explain your classroom rules.

Clearly explain each of your classroom rules. Very briefly talk about why each rule is necessary and why you have chosen it. For example, the rule "Be in your seat when the bell rings" is necessary to make sure that lessons begin on time. By beginning lessons on time, you will be able to cover the material your students need to be successful in school.

3 Check for understanding.

Take the time to make sure that all students understand the rules you've taught. Ask if there are any questions and make sure that students understand that these rules are in effect at all times—during all activities.

4 Explain why you have consequences.

Explain to students that only they are responsible for the behavioral choices they make. They need to know that when they choose to break a rule, they will also be choosing to receive a consequence. Explain that whenever one makes poor choices in life, there are often consequences to those choices. It's true in the workplace, it's true at home, and it's true in school.

> "What would happen if you showed up late for work?"
> "What would your boss do if you decided to behave inappropriately on the job?"

5 Explain the consequences.

Tell students exactly what will happen if they choose to break a rule once in a class period, twice in the period, three times, four times and five times in a period. Explain how you will keep track of consequences.

(Hold up clipboard.) "I'm going to keep this clipboard near me throughout the class period. The first time you break a rule, I will write your name down on the clipboard. I'll also remind you of what the rule is. For

example, if I hear a student swearing in the classroom, I will say, for example, 'John, the rule is no swearing. That is a warning.'

"That's all that I'll do.

"This warning gives you a second chance to choose appropriate behavior. Use this signal wisely so that you can avoid any further consequences.

"If you do break this rule again, or any other rule during the class period, I'll circle the '2' on the chart. This means that you've broken a rule two times, even if it's not the same rule, and that you have chosen to stay after class for one minute. I know one minute doesn't sound like a lot of time, but your friends will not be permitted to wait for you, and you will not be allowed to talk to anyone or move out of your seat until that minute is up. This will give you time to think about your behavior and plan to behave more appropriately the next time you come to class.

"The third time you break a rule, you will stay after class for two minutes and complete a Behavior Journal sheet which you will take home and have signed by your parent (*optional*)." (Give students a step-by-step explanation for completing the Behavior Journal sheet.)

Go through the rest of your disciplinary hierarchy in this manner, explaining each consequence. Afterwards, take the time to emphasize your belief that the students can behave appropriately and make responsible choices for themselves.

"I know that all of you can follow our classroom rules. I know that all of you can make good decisions when you enter the room, when you speak, when you do your work, and when you interact with your classmates. I hope that you won't have to experience disciplinary consequences, and that I won't have to call your parents or speak to the (dean) about problems. By making responsible choices you can make this your most successful and enjoyable year yet."

6 Check for understanding

It's important that all students clearly understand the consequences you will use in your classroom. Ask students if they have any questions.

7 Explain how you will reinforce students who follow the rules.

Positive reinforcement is going to be the most important part of your classroom discipline plan. Tell your students again that you know they can all be successful at following the classroom rules, and that throughout the year you will recognize and reward those students who follow the rules. Pique student enthusiasm by detailing the positive reinforcement you will use. Increase interest further by asking students to suggest positive ideas that they'd like to see used.

"See these 'You've Earned It' coupons? From time to time I'll be giving these coupons to students who follow the rules and follow directions. I will be filling in the coupons with special privileges you would like to earn."

Keep this in mind: The manner in which you present your discipline plan to your students will set the tone for your classroom for the entire year. Be positive! Communicate your high expectations. Emphasize to your students that you believe they will choose to follow the rules and enjoy the rewards of their good behavior. However, students must also understand that if they choose to break a rule, a consequence will follow.

Refer to pages 97-110 of the revised Assertive Discipline text for additional sample scripts for teaching this lesson.

It's Your Turn

Teaching your classroom discipline plan is an important lesson, one that will impact your classroom environment for the rest of the year. Take the time to carefully plan the lesson. Use the Lesson-Planning Worksheet on the following pages as you organize your lesson.

TEACHING YOUR CLASSROOM DISCIPLINE PLAN

LESSON PLANNING WORKSHEET

1. Explain why you need rules in the classroom.

_____

_____

_____

_____

2. Explain the rules.

_____

_____

_____

_____

3. Check for understanding.

_____

_____

_____

_____

4. Explain why you have consequences.

_____

_____

_____

_____

5. Explain the consequences.

_____

_____

_____

_____

_____

_____

6. Explain how you will reinforce students who choose to follow the rules.

_____

_____

_____

_____

_____

_____

7. Check for understanding.

_____

_____

_____

_____

_____

_____

After you've taught the lesson. . .

Don't wait even one day, or one period, to start reinforcing students for following your classroom rules. As soon as the lesson has been taught, look for opportunities to recognize students for responsible behavior and immediately begin reinforcing students who follow the rules.

Let students know that you notice and appreciate the good efforts they're making. Through your actions let them know that you mean what you said about positive reinforcement.

"William, thank you for being in your seat before the bell rang."

It's Your Turn

The ideas that follow will help you reinforce students' appropriate behavior at the start of the year.

"Great Start" Raffle Tickets

Reinforce good habits by awarding Great Start Raffle Tickets to students who exhibit responsible behavior during the first weeks of school. When a student receives a ticket he or she signs and deposits it in the class collection box. Once a week (or however often you determine) a designated number of tickets are drawn and prizes or privileges given. This activity will motivate students to develop the responsible habits that will help them succeed all year long.

Try this: Encourage your students to start smart right at the start! Tell students that you will be awarding raffle tickets to those who return the signed discipline plan to school on time. Then hold a special drawing just for those students.

Students of the Week Bulletin Board

Recognize responsible behavior and effort all year long by putting the spotlight on different students each week. At the start of the year explain that every week you will select one student from each class to be Student of the Week. The honor will include being highlighted on a Students of the Week Bulletin Board (students contribute photographs of themselves with family and friends) plus any special privilege or recognition you may wish to add.

Here's what to do:

1. Collect magazine covers to use as frames for students' photographs. *People*, *Sports Illustrated*, *Rolling Stone*, *Newsweek* and *Time* all make terrific backdrops for photos.

The more eclectic a supply you gather, the more personalized your frames can be. (For example, a student who's a cyclist would enjoy being placed on the cover of *Bicycling*. A budding rock musician would prefer *Rolling Stone*.) Cover the fronts of the magazines with construction paper, leaving just the mastheads showing.

2. Reproduce copies of the "Student of the Week" stars (page 68) on bright yellow or gold paper. Keep a supply handy so that each week you can write the name of each honored student in his or her own star.

3. Introduce the program to students, explaining that students who are selected as Student of the Week (on Friday) can bring photographs of themselves, family, friends to school Monday to be displayed on the bulletin board.

4. Keep an instant camera at school to take pictures of any student who may not be able to contribute photographs.

5. Create the bulletin board by adding headline lettering: "Students of the Week." Each week add new photographs to the magazine frames and pin up on the board with personalized stars.

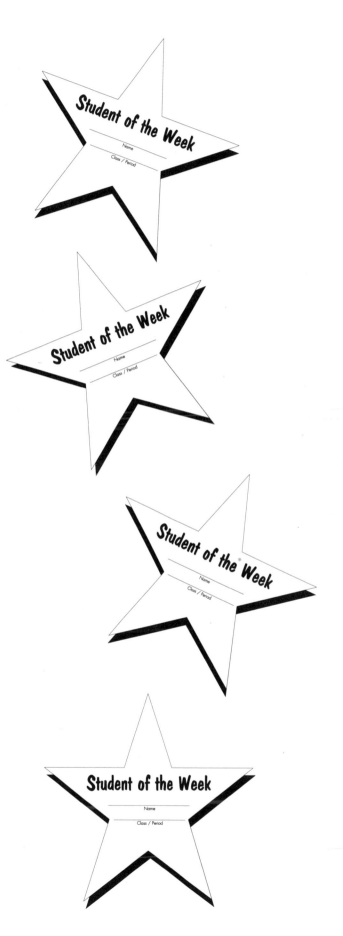

Post rules reminders.

On pages 69-72 you will find posters of general rules that are commonly found in secondary classrooms. If these rules are part of your plan, run them off on brightly colored paper (fluorescent or neon would get attention) and display them in the room.

An open-ended bordered poster is also included to use for other rules of your own, as well as a "Be Cool—Follow the Rules" poster that's applicable to any classroom.

Why post rules? For the same reason they're posted in offices, factories and any working environment: To serve as a reminder of expectations.

Post your plan.

Display the Rules, Positive Recognition and Consequences posters in your classroom as an ever-present reminder of your classroom discipline plan. (This is important information for students, classroom visitors, new students, and substitutes, too.)

For the record . . .

Record your beginning-of-the-year classroom discipline plan lesson on a cassette tape. When new students arrive in your classroom they won't be at a disadvantage—they can hear that all-important lesson firsthand! Make sure that new students receive a copy of the discipline plan letter to take home to parents (see pages 75-76).

And as the year proceeds. . .

Review your classroom rules frequently at the start of the year. Review as needed as the year progresses. It's especially important to review classroom rules after vacations and on days when students are excited about special events (the day before or after a holiday, or the day of a dance or big game).

GREAT START
Raffle Ticket

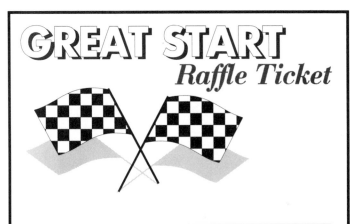

NAME   CLASS/PERIOD

GREAT START
Raffle Ticket

NAME   CLASS/PERIOD

GREAT START
Raffle Ticket

NAME   CLASS/PERIOD

GREAT START
Raffle Ticket

NAME   CLASS/PERIOD

GREAT START
Raffle Ticket

NAME   CLASS/PERIOD

GREAT START
Raffle Ticket

NAME   CLASS/PERIOD

GREAT START
Raffle Ticket

NAME   CLASS/PERIOD

GREAT START
Raffle Ticket

NAME   CLASS/PERIOD

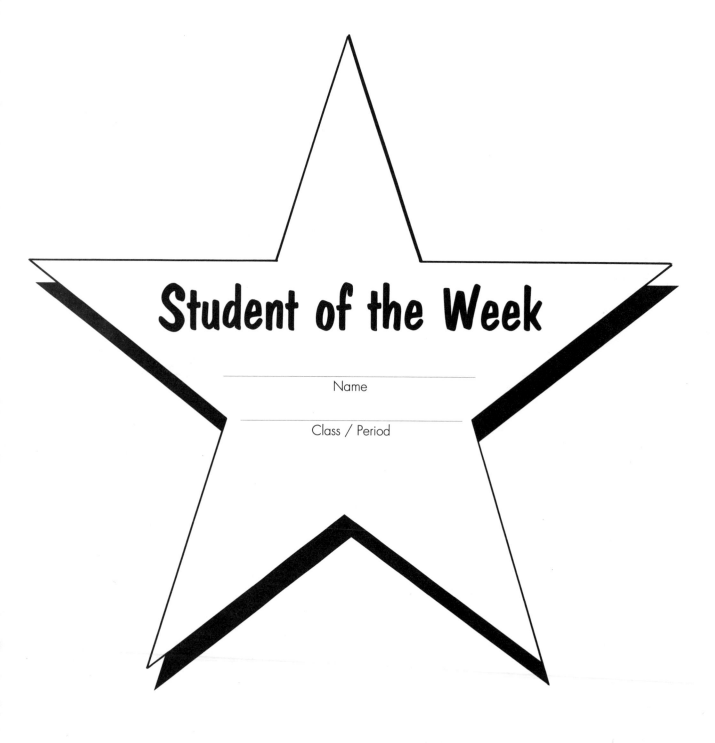

Student of the Week

_____

Name

_____

Class / Period

CLASSROOM Rule

Follow directions.

CLASSROOM Rule

Keep hands, feet and objects to yourself.

CLASSROOM Rule

Do not leave the room without permission.

CLASSROOM Rule

Bring all required materials to class each day.

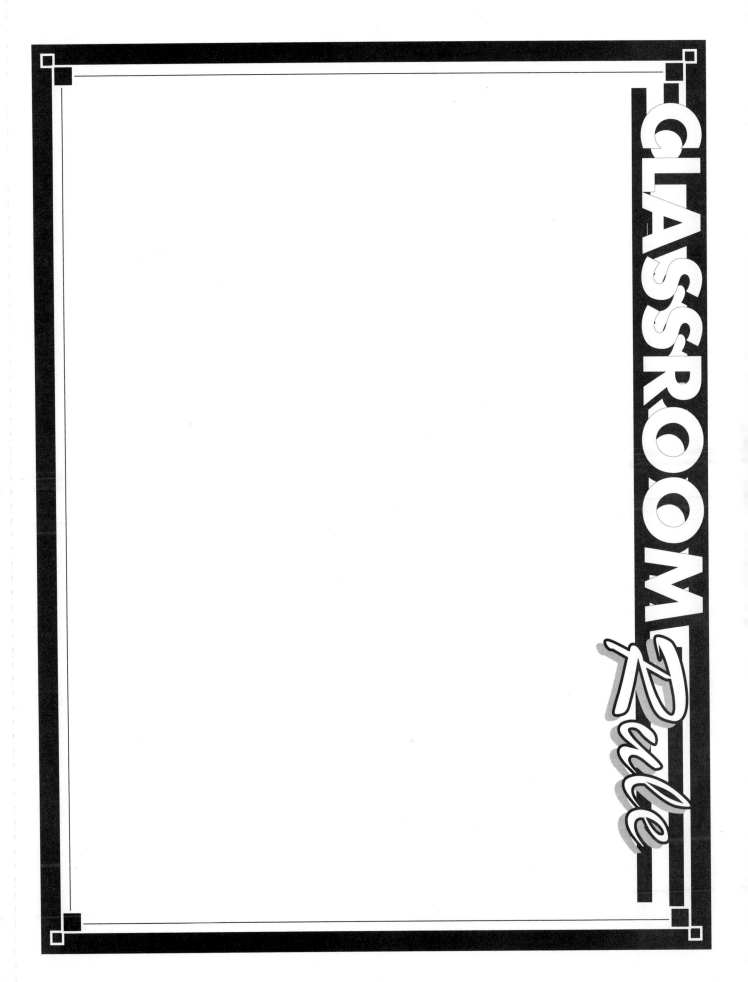

CLASSROOM Rule

Send Home a Copy of Your Discipline Plan to Parents

If parents are to become partners in their children's education, they must be well-informed about your classroom discipline plan. After all, contacting parents is part of your discipline hierarchy, and you want them to be supportive when you need them. Parents, therefore, need to be informed about why you have a plan and your rationale for rules, positive reinforcement and consequences.

Give each student a copy of your discipline plan to take home to parents (or, if the budget allows, mail the plan home). In a letter, explain why a classroom discipline plan is important, and ask parents to go over the plan with their children. Have parents and student sign and return a statement at the bottom that verifies that they have read the plan, discussed it together, and will support the plan. Keep the signed statements on file.

Tell your students:

"Before you leave today, you will receive a copy of this letter to your parents that explains our classroom discipline plan. I want you to show the plan to your parents and make sure that they understand what we've talked about in class today. After you have talked about the plan, I want you *and* your parents to sign the bottom of the sheet. Please bring the tear-off portion back to me. I want all of your parents to know what I expect of you in this class. And I want them to know that we will work together to make sure this is a successful year for all of you."

Your letter to parents should include the following:

- Your reason for having a classroom discipline plan.

- A list of the rules, positive reinforcement and consequences that are included in your plan.

- A message asking parents to support your discipline plan.

- An invitation for parents to call you with any concerns they might wish to discuss.

- An acknowledgement statement to be signed by parent(s) and student.

- Space for comments.

Review your discipline plan with parents at Back-to-School Night. It's the perfect opportunity to discuss classroom rules, positive reinforcement and consequences, and to answer any questions parents may have.

It's Your Turn

Copy your discipline plan on the letterhead on page 77. Use the sample letter on page 76 as a guide for writing your own letter. Reproduce and distribute to parents. Make extra copies to keep on file for new students who enter your class during the school year.

Substitute Support

There will be times when you won't be able to be at school—illness, meetings, etc. But you can make sure that your classes continue to run smoothly and productively—no matter who is in charge. To ensure consistent behavior management in your classroom, even when you are not present, prepare a discipline plan for substitutes. Fill in your discipline plan on the Substitute Sheet on page 78. Make sure that a copy is left in the office. Put another copy in your lesson plan book or tape it to the top of your desk. If your plan is different in any respect for different classes, make sure you clearly designate this. Stress to students that responsible behavior is expected when a substitute takes over—the discipline plan is in effect no matter who is teaching.

It is also important that any paraprofessionals who work in your room understand the discipline plan and the role they are to play in its implementation. Take time to explain the plan.

Classroom Plan

Dear Parent,

I am delighted that _____ is in my (political science, English, Geometry) class this year. With your encouragement, your child will participate in and enjoy many exciting and rewarding experiences this academic year.

Since lifelong success depends in part on learning to make responsible choices, I have developed a classroom discipline plan which guides every student to make good decisions about his or her behavior. Your child deserves the most positive educational climate possible for his/her growth, and I know that together we will make a difference in this process. The plan below outlines our classroom rules, positive recognition for appropriate behavior and consequences for inappropriate behavior. They are:

Rules: 1. Follow directions.
            2. Keep hands, feet and objects to yourself.
            3. No swearing, teasing or name calling.
            4. Be in your seat when the bell rings

Positive Recognition:
To encourage students to follow these classroom rules, I will recognize appropriate behavior with praise, "good news" notes home and positive phone calls home.

Consequences:
If a student chooses to break a rule, however, the following steps will be taken:

First time a student breaks a rule:	Warning
Second time:	Stay one minute after class
Third time:	Stay two minutes after class and complete a Behavior Journal sheet
Fourth time:	Call parents
Fifth time:	Send to vice principal
Severe Disruption	Send to vice principal

Be assured that my goal is to work with you to ensure the success of your child this year. Please read and discuss this classroom discipline plan with your child, then sign and return the form below. Feel free to call me anytime you'd like to talk something over.

Sincerely,

- -

I have read the discipline plan and have discussed it with my child, _____.

Parent/Guardian Signature_____ Date_____

Student Signature_____

Comments:_____

_____

_____

SUBSTITUTE'S PLAN

From the desk of: _____

Dear Substitute:

Listed below are the guidelines for the discipline plan used in my classroom. My students know the rules. They understand that these rules are in effect at all times, and they know the consequences that will occur should they break the rules of the classroom.

Please follow these guidelines exactly, and leave me a list of any students who break the rules.

Classroom Rules

1 _____
2 _____
3 _____
4 _____

Consequences

When a student breaks a rule:
1st time _____
2nd time _____
3rd time _____
4th time _____
5th time _____

Severe Clause: If a student exhibits severe misbehavior such as fighting, open defiance or vulgar language, the following consequence is to be immediately imposed: _____

Please offer plenty of praise and positive recognition to students who follow the rules. They'll appreciate it, and your praise will help encourage other students to cooperate, too!

Thank you for following my classroom discipline plan.

Sincerely,

SECTION THREE

Teaching Responsible Behavior

Developing your classroom discipline plan and teaching this plan to your students are the first steps you take to help them choose the responsible behavior that will enable them to succeed in school.

The next step is to teach your students how to make responsible behavioral choices in all situations at school.

In this section of the *Assertive Discipline Secondary Workbook* we will look at a variety of techniques that will help you motivate the majority of your students to behave appropriately.

Also included in this section is a selection of reproducibles that will help you implement these techniques.

Determining and Teaching Specific Directions

Your classroom discipline plan lists the general rules of your classroom. As you have seen, these rules are in effect at all times.

The most important of these classroom rules is, "Follow directions." This rule is included to ensure that students promptly follow *any* direction you might give during the class period.

To comply with this rule, students must understand what each specific direction you give means. You can never assume that a classroom full of students will all follow a direction in the same way. After all, your students have 5 to 7 teachers each day—each with different procedures and routines to follow.

- Do your students know how you expect them to participate during a class discussion?

- Do they know how you expect them to conduct themselves during a lecture?

- Do they know how you expect them to enter and leave the room?

There are many ways to go about following any direction. If you want all your students to follow a direction in the same way, you must teach them what you expect. Right at the beginning of the year you need to take the time to teach your students exactly how you want them to behave in all classroom situations. You need to teach and reteach your expectations until every student knows how to enter and leave the classroom, how to behave during a lecture, and how to work in groups.

Remember, the goal is for all of your students to succeed.

The more time you spend at the beginning of the year clarifying your specific directions, the less time you'll spend *repeating* them as the year goes by.

Here's what to do:

First, identify the academic activities, routine procedures and special procedures for which specific directions are needed.

Next, determine the specific directions you want your students to follow for each activity and procedure you've identified.

Here are examples of academic activities:

- When you are giving a directed lesson in front of the class

- When students are doing independent work

- When students are working in small groups doing cooperative learning tasks

- When the class is having a group discussion

- When students are taking a test

- When students are working at independent lab stations

- When a student is making a presentation to the class

Here are examples of routine procedures:

- When students enter the classroom
- When students are dismissed
- When a student needs to use the restroom
- When a student needs to sharpen a pencil
- When students turn in homework
- When the teacher gives a signal to begin an activity
- When students transition from one activity to another
- When the teacher is taking attendance
- When the phone rings or a PA announcement is heard
- When students are putting away equipment
- When students are cleaning up
- When students are viewing movies in class

Special Procedures

- When guests come to the classroom
- Emergency procedures

    Note: Music teachers, art teachers, PE teachers and teachers who work in other special situations should develop a list of the activities and procedures that apply to their students.

For example:

- Putting music equipment away
- Putting sports equipment away
- Cleaning up after an art activity

The Difference Between Rules and Directions

- **Rules** are posted in your classroom, and are in effect at all times during the day.

- **Directions** are in effect for the duration of a specific activity. Directions may change based on the needs of the teacher and maturity level of the students.

It's Your Turn

Now think about a typical week in your own classroom. Start at Period 1 on Monday and work your way through to the end of the day on Friday. Identify the academic activities, routine procedures and special procedures the students in each of your classes will be engaged in. Try not to leave anything out. List all of these on the Specific Directions Worksheet on page 82.

SPECIFIC DIRECTIONS WORKSHEET

Use this worksheet to list all the academic activities, routine procedures and special procedures that occur during the school week.

Academic Activities

Routine Procedures

Special Procedures

SPECIFIC DIRECTIONS WORKSHEET

Use this worksheet to list all the academic activities, routine procedures and special procedures that occur during the school week.

Academic Activities

- _____
- _____
- _____
- _____
- _____
- _____

- _____
- _____
- _____
- _____
- _____
- _____

Routine Procedures

- _____
- _____
- _____
- _____
- _____
- _____

- _____
- _____
- _____
- _____
- _____
- _____

Special Procedures

- _____
- _____
- _____
- _____
- _____
- _____

- _____
- _____
- _____
- _____
- _____
- _____

Now, determine the specific directions you want your students to follow.

After you've listed all the activities for which you need specific directions, it's time to decide on those directions. When determining the specific directions you want your students to follow, use these guidelines:

- **Keep it simple!**

Choose a limited number of directions for each classroom activity.

- **Choose directions that are observable.**

Your directions must be observable and easy for students to follow. Don't include vague directions such as "act good" or "behave appropriately."

- **Relate your directions to:**

  1 How you want students to participate in the activity or procedure—*what you expect them to do.*

  2 How you expect students to *behave* in order to be successful in the activity.

Here are some examples of specific directions:

Academic Activity: When the teacher is giving a lecture.

1 Clear your desks of everything but notebook and pencil.

2 Eyes on me, or eyes on your paper. Take notes on the lecture. No talking while I'm talking.

(These directions let students know what they are expected to do.)

3 Raise your hand and wait to be called upon to ask or answer a question or make a comment.

(This direction lets students know how you expect them to behave.)

Academic Activity: When students are working independently.

1 Have all necessary books, paper, pencils and other materials on your desk.

2 Begin working on your assignment as soon as you receive it.

(These directions let students know what they are expected to do.)

3 No talking. Raise your hand to ask a question.

(This direction lets students know how you expect them to behave.)

Routine Procedure: When students enter the classroom.

1 Walk into the room.

2 Go directly to your seat and sit down.

(These directions let students know what they are expected to do.)

3 No talking after the bell rings.

(This direction lets students know how you expect them to behave.)

Special Procedure: Assemblies

1 Put books and materials away.

2 When your row (or section) is called, line up at the door in single file without talking. Remember to walk.

3 Without talking, walk to the auditorium.

4 No talking during the assembly.

5 Return to class in a single line. No talking. Go directly to your seat and sit down.

It's Your Turn

Write the specific directions for the classroom activities that apply to your own teaching situation. We've started the list with some activities that generally take place in all classrooms. Add to this list as needed.

Activity: When students enter the classroom

1 _____

2 _____

3 _____

Activity: When you are giving a directed lesson

1 _____

2 _____

3 _____

Activity: When the class is involved in a class discussion

1 _____

2 _____

3 _____

Activity: When students are taking a test

1 _____

2 _____

3 _____

Activity: When students turn in homework

1 _____

2 _____

3 _____

Activity: When students leave the classroom at the end of the period

1 _____

2 _____

3 _____

Now write directions for any other classroom activities you listed on page 82.

Activity: _____

1 _____

2 _____

3 _____

Activity: _____

1 _____

2 _____

3 _____

Activity: _____

1 _____

2 _____

3 _____

Activity: _____

1 _____

2 _____

3 _____

Activity: _____

1 _____

2 _____

3 _____

Activity: _____

1 _____

2 _____

3 _____

Activity: _____

1 _____

2 _____

3 _____

Teach your specific directions.

Once you've determined your specific directions, your goal in teaching them is not to simply pass along instructions, but to make this process a learning experience for your students as well.

Teach students *why* your directions are important to cooperation and successful learning. When your students understand the need to follow directions, they can take ownership of the expectations you hold for the class and will be better able to meet those expectations.

Why teach specific directions with such care?

Here are two good reasons:

• Teaching your specific directions ensures that behavior problems will be reduced during all academic activities, routine procedures and special procedures.

• Teaching specific directions increases a student's opportunity to succeed at those activities.

As with any successful lesson, preparation is vital to meeting your objectives. The lesson sequence on this page highlights points you'll want to include in your own specific directions lessons. Use this lesson as a guideline for developing a lesson for any specific direction. Keep in mind that your own lessons will differ, based on the age and maturity of your students and the directions you are teaching, but the three main areas of focus—**explanation, teaching** and **checking for understanding**—remain the same.

Here's a sample lesson sequence for teaching the specific directions for taking a quiz.

1 Explain the rationale for the direction.

Students need to understand why your directions are important. Briefly explain why students need to follow the direction and what the benefit will be to them and to other students.

"At the end of class each Friday I will give the direction to get ready for a weekly quiz. It's important to follow the direction so that you will be able to complete the quiz on time, and do well in this class."

2 Involve students by asking questions.

Students will follow your directions more readily if you involve them in a discussion that rationally addresses your concerns.

"What would happen if we waste a lot of time getting ready for the quiz?"

3 Explain the specific directions.

Now teach students the directions they will be expected to follow. Remind them that when everyone follows these directions, all students will have an opportunity to succeed in class.

"These are the directions you need to follow whenever I announce a quiz.

"When I say the words, "Friday quiz," I want you to clear your desks, except for a pen. No talking. When you receive your quiz sheet, leave it face down on your desk until I tell you to begin.

"When I say 'Begin,' turn your paper right-side up, write your name and the date and begin taking the quiz. No talking. No getting out of your seat. If you have a question, raise your hand and I'll come over to you.

"When you're finished, check over your answers and turn the sheet over. You may take out a book and read silently until the papers are collected."

4 Check for understanding.

Check for understanding by asking students to restate the directions. Then reinforce the directions further by writing them on the board or presenting them on an overhead. At this point you may also want to have students copy the specific directions to keep for reference.

After you've taught a specific directions lesson . . .

Immediately follow up any specific directions lesson with the activity or procedure that has just been taught. (In the previous example, the teacher would actually then give students the quiz.) Be sure to reinforce students who follow the directions appropriately, and give reminders to (or reteach if necessary) those students who are having difficulty.

Guidelines for Reviewing Specific Directions

First Two Weeks
Review directions each time the class engages in the activity.

First Month
Review directions each Monday (as a reminder and refresher for the week to come).

Remainder of Year
Review directions as needed. It is especially important to review directions after a vacation, on special days when students are excited (day before a vacation, the day of a dance or major school event).

Refer to pages 128-136 of the revised Assertive Discipline text for additional guidelines for teaching specific directions to your students.

It's Your Turn

Here are some ideas that will help you teach specific directions to your students.

Plan your lessons.
Use the Specific Directions Planning Sheet on pages 89-90 to plan the lessons you will teach. Make plenty of copies and use them to write down points you want to make and other reminders to yourself.

LESSON PLAN FOR TEACHING
SPECIFIC DIRECTIONS

Objective: To teach specific directions for_____

When to present this lesson: Teach directions for this activity prior to the first time the activity takes place.

These are the specific directions I will teach for this activity.

_____
_____
_____
_____
_____

Now, plan the lesson you will teach.

Explain the rationale for the direction:

_____
_____
_____
_____
_____
_____
_____
_____
_____
_____
_____
_____

Post your directions.

Visual reminders can often help students remember directions. Use the open-ended bordered poster on page 91 to create handy reminders of some of your more commonly given (or most important) directions.

"Cue Words" will cue students!

Students will follow directions more quickly and easily if you tie your directions to a cue word that you always say when giving the direction.

For example:

"When I say the words 'quiz time,' I expect you to . . . ."

"When I say the words 'lab partners,' I expect you to . . . ."

"When I say the words 'clean up,' I expect you to . . . ."

"When I say the words 'take notes,' I expect you to . . . ."

"When I count to three, I expect you to . . . ."

"When I say 'go,' I expect you to . . . ."

Create a Classroom Directions Binder

As new students enter your class throughout the year, they too will need to learn your specific directions. Here's an idea that can help ease their transition and involve peers in the teaching process:

Use the open-ended "Directions for " worksheet on page 91 to create a list of directions for different activities.

Organize these sheets into a looseleaf binder. When a new student joins the class, assign him or her a student guide. It's the responsibility of the guide to go through the binder with the new student and explain each of these directions.

The binder can also be used to reteach students who repeatedly receive warnings or consequences for not following directions. Have the student read and copy the specific directions he or she is having trouble with to help reinforce his or her understanding of the directions.

LESSON PLAN FOR TEACHING
SPECIFIC DIRECTIONS

Objective: To teach specific directions for_____

When to present this lesson: Teach directions for this activity prior to the first
time the activity takes place.

These are the specific directions I will teach for this activity.

_____
_____
_____
_____
_____

Now, plan the lesson you will teach.

Explain the rationale for the direction:

_____
_____
_____
_____
_____
_____
_____
_____
_____
_____
_____
_____
_____
_____
_____
_____
_____

Involve the students by asking questions:

_____
_____
_____
_____
_____
_____
_____

Explain the specific directions:

_____
_____
_____
_____
_____
_____
_____

Check for understanding:

_____
_____
_____
_____

Notes on the lesson:

_____
_____
_____
_____
_____
_____
_____

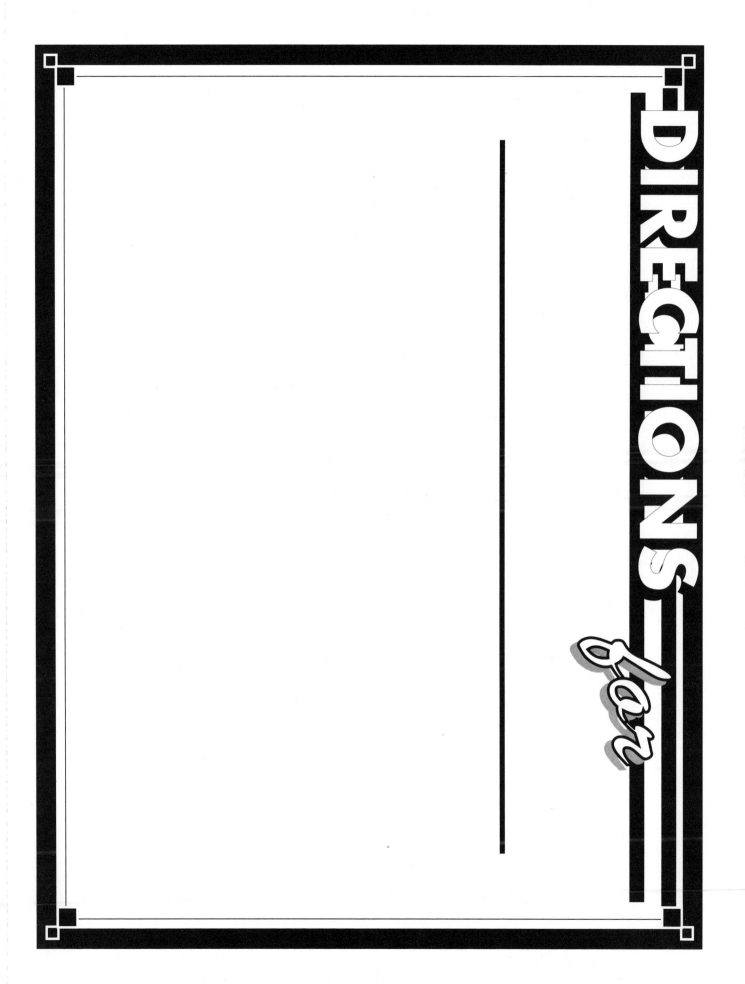

DIRECTIONS for

Teaching Responsible Behavior
Using Positive Recognition to Motivate Students to Behave

Once you've taught your students directions for all classroom activities, your goal is to help them be successful in following those directions.

Positive recognition is the most effective way to achieve this goal.

We will give you a variety of techniques that you can use to motivate students to choose appropriate behavior and then to *continue* that behavior.

These techniques are:

1 Positive Repetition

2 Consistent Praise

3 Scanning

4 Circulating the Classroom

On the following pages you will learn how to use each of these techniques throughout the day—while you teach, and while you are involved in any classroom activity.

Keep positive recognition techniques at your fingertips with Assertive Discipline Cue Cards.

What are Assertive Discipline Cue Cards?

Cue Cards are a quick and easy way to keep Assertive Discipline techniques close at hand and in your mind. All of the positive recognition techniques listed in this chapter, and other behavior management techniques included in upcoming chapters, have been organized into easy-to-use Assertive Discipline Cue Cards.

These reproducible Cue Cards give you portable, to-the-point references for successfully handling both appropriate and inappropriate classroom behavior.

Here are some guidelines for using the Cue Cards:

• **Read**

Read each Cue Card. Take time to think about how you can use each of these techniques in the day-to-day routines of your classes.

• **Keep**

Laminate the Cue Cards and then tuck them into your lesson plan book for easy reference. From time to time review the techniques and make sure you are using them—effectively *and* consistently.

• **Share**

Give a set of Cue Cards to any other personnel or volunteers who work in your classroom. Encourage them to read the cards and use the techniques with students.

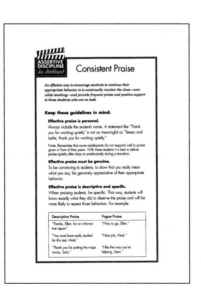

Positive Repetition

This technique will help encourage students to follow the many directions you give each day. It's called positive repetition.

Here's how positive repetition works:

1   Give a direction.

2   Immediately look for groups, rows or clusters of students who are following the direction.

3   Identify those groups and restate the direction as they are following it.

Examples:

Direction:
"Please turn to the notes you took yesterday on Shakespeare."
Positive Repetition:
"Everyone in row three has their notes out and is ready for review."

Direction:
"Please move into your debate teams."
Positive Repetition:
"Jason, Carly and Rita are with their team. Great!"

CUE CARD # 1

Guidelines for Frequency of Positive Repetition

At the beginning of the year you will be placing a heavy emphasis on teaching students how to behave and follow your directions. The more you want to teach students how to behave, the more you need to use praise. Thus, at the beginning of the year you will use positive repetition much more frequently than you will once your students learn what you need them to do in each classroom situation. Remember, one of the goals of positive reinforcement is to start strong, then gradually decrease the frequency.

As the year proceeds, use this technique as needed to help students get on task.

Positive repetition is a positive advantage for you and your students!

You give hundreds of directions in a week. And each time you give a direction you have a ready-made opportunity to positively reinforce students. When you get into the habit of using this technique, you will be assured that you will make more positive than negative statements to students.

Consistent Praise

An effective way to encourage students to continue their appropriate behavior is to continually monitor the class—even while teaching—and provide frequent praise and positive support to those students who are on task.

Keep these guidelines in mind:

Effective praise is personal.

Always include the student's name. A statement like "Thank you for working quietly" is not as meaningful as "Teresa and Leslie, thank you for working quietly."

Note: Remember that some adolescents do not respond well to praise given in front of their peers. With these students it is best to deliver praise quietly after class or unobtrusively during a transition.

Effective praise must be genuine.

To be convincing to students, to show that you really mean what you say, be genuinely appreciative of their appropriate behavior.

Effective praise is descriptive and specific.

When praising students, be specific. That way, students will know exactly what they did to deserve the praise and will be more likely to repeat those behaviors. For example:

Descriptive Praise	Vague Praise
"Thanks, Ellen, for an informative report."	"Way to go, Ellen."
"You must have really studied for this test, Mark."	"Nice job, Mark."
"Thank you for putting the maps away, Sara."	"I like the way you're helping, Sara."

CUE CARD # 2

ASSERTIVE DISCIPLINE in Action!

Scanning

The scanning technique is useful when you are working with a small group of students, or an individual student, and the rest of the class is working independently. The objective of this technique is to reinforce students who are on task, thereby encouraging them to remain on task. This technique will help you recognize students who normally may not receive attention until they misbehave. By using this technique, you can keep independent workers on task and still remain working with one small group.

Here's how to use the scanning technique:

1 When you are working with a small group, look up every few minutes and scan the students who are working independently.

2 As you notice students who are working appropriately, take a moment to recognize their good behavior.

"The group near the window has been working nonstop on the assignment. Thank you!"

3 The students will appreciate the recognition and continue working independently. Other students will get the message that you are aware of what's going on in the room, and will be motivated to stay on task themselves.

Note: Secondary students typically do not like to be singled out for praise in front of the entire class. Praising a group of students, as in the example above, is far more effective.

CUE CARD # 3

ASSERTIVE DISCIPLINE
in Action!

Circulating the Classroom

While students are working independently, circulate the room and give positive recognition. One-on-one, you can quietly and unobtrusively let a student know that you recognize his or her appropriate behavior. This positive recognition is given quietly— a special message from the teacher to the student.

"Cliff, this is going to be a terrific speech. This first line will really grab your audience!"

"Marianna, you've really been working hard all period, and your assignment is just about finished. Good work!"

There is no need to ever phase out this technique. Each time you circulate the classroom you have an opportunity to show your students you care, and that you notice their good efforts.

CUE CARD # 4

Teaching Responsible Behavior
Redirecting Non-disruptive Off-task Behavior

By giving your students consistent positive recognition, you can eliminate the majority of problems before they even begin.

Experience has most likely shown you, however, that there still will be students who behave inappropriately. This behavior can take two forms: disruptive off-task behavior and non-disruptive off-task behavior.

Disruptive Off-task Behaviors

Shouting out in class

Throwing spit balls

Pushing or shoving

Slamming books on the desk

Moving around the room

Non-disruptive Off-task Behaviors

Looking out the window

Reading instead of listening

Daydreaming

Doodling instead of working

Putting head on desk or sleeping

We will take a closer look at disruptive off-task behavior, and how to deal with it, on pages 104-105. Now we will focus on how to respond to non-disruptive off-task behavior—behavior in which a student is not disrupting others, but is not paying attention or staying on task, either.

As any teacher knows, students frequently fall into non-disruptive off-task behavior. After all, it doesn't take much for a 16-year-old to lose interest in class and start doodling on his paper, or to stare out the window instead of listening to a lecture.

The teacher's responsibility is to guide the student back into learning.

Here's what you *don't* want to do:

1) ignore the behavior or

2) give an immediate consequence.

Ignoring the behavior doesn't get the student back on task, and therefore the student isn't participating or learning.

Giving an immediate consequence in many cases is an overreaction to a simple lapse of attention.

Here's what you *do* want to do:

Calmly, and with caring guidance, give the student an opportunity to get back on task.

It's Your Turn

The Assertive Discipline Cue Cards on pages 100-103 contain four techniques that will help you redirect a student's non-disruptive off-task behavior *while you continue to teach*. Read each technique and imagine how you can use it throughout the day to nudge students back into your lessons. Reproduce these Cue Cards, laminate them, and keep them nearby for easy and frequent review.

1 The Look

2 Physical Proximity

3 Mention Name

4 Proximity Praise

Once a student is back on track?

As soon as a student is back on task, take advantage of the opportunity to praise his or her behavior. Let the student know that paying attention in class earns positive recognition.

How often do you redirect?

How many times should you redirect a student before you start giving consequences? Obviously you can't go on redirecting a student over and over within a class period. At some point you may have to turn to consequences.

Here's a rule of thumb:

When you find yourself having to redirect a student twice in a period you can assume that the student is not receiving enough structure to help him control his behavior. In these situations, turn to your disciplinary hierarchy and issue a warning.

If the off-task behavior still continues, you may need to proceed further and use consequences from your disciplinary hierarchy.

> Note: If the non-disruptive off-task behavior seems out of character for a student, something might be wrong that you need to know about. Before turning to consequences, take the student aside and, in a caring manner, say (for example), "It seems like you're having difficulty paying attention in class today. Would you like to talk about it?"

Always remember that your own good judgment is your most valuable guide in assessing student behavior.

The "Look"

Just giving a look that says, "I'm aware of and disapprove of your behavior" is an effective way of redirecting some non-disruptive off-task behaviors.

Here's how this technique works:

Instead of attentively listening to a history lecture, Laurie aimlessly sits tipping her chair back on two legs. When the teacher notices Laurie's off-task behavior, she makes direct eye contact with her and looks at her with a firm, calm look on her face. She maintains this eye contact until Laurie puts all four legs of her chair on the floor and begins to take notes.

CUE CARD # 5

Physical Proximity

Sometimes you don't even have to say a word to redirect a student back on task. Simply walk over and stand close by the student. The student will know why you've arrived at his or her side and will respond.

Here's an example of physical proximity at work:

While reading a magazine article to the class, the teacher notices that Terry has put his head down on his desk and has "tuned out." Continuing to read, the teacher walks back to Terry and stands near his desk, putting her hand on the back of his chair, while she proceeds with the article. As soon as Terry becomes aware of his teacher's presence, he lifts his head and starts paying attention.

CUE CARD # 6

ASSERTIVE DISCIPLINE *in Action!*

Mention the off-task student's name while teaching.

Just mentioning a student's name while you are teaching a lesson may be enough to redirect his or her attention back on task.

Here's an example of a teacher using this technique:

While pointing to a map during a geography lesson, the teacher notices that Christine is off task and not paying attention. The teacher, in a very matter-of-fact manner, continues the lesson saying, "All right, now suppose Christine lives in Papua, New Guinea, and she wants to travel to Sydney, Australia to see her friend, Greg . . . ."

As soon as Christine's name is mentioned, she looks up, tunes in, and immediately begins paying attention.

CUE CARD # 7

ASSERTIVE DISCIPLINE in Action!

Proximity Praise

An effective way to redirect a non-disruptive off-task student back on task is to focus on the appropriate behavior of those students around him.

Here's an example of a teacher using proximity praise:

The entire class, with the exception of Alex, is working independently on their research reports. Rather than doing his report, Alex is idly doodling pictures in his notebook. On either side of Alex, Tawny and Colin are both doing their work. Wanting to get Alex on task, the teacher says, "Tawny and Colin, you both look like you're really into your research. Good job."

As she expects, Alex looks around him, notices what is going on and gets back to work.

This technique is doubly effective. Off-task students are motivated to get back on task, and students who are on task receive well-deserved praise.

CUE CARD # 8

Implementing Consequences

We have talked about the importance of secondary students learning to accept responsibility for the behavior choices they make. As part of this learning, students need to understand that negative consequences are a natural outcome of misbehavior.

When students disrupt and keep you from teaching, or other students from learning, you will have to follow through with consequences.

On page 48 you learned to develop a discipline hierarchy as part of your classroom discipline plan. How you use the consequences in the hierarchy will determine its success in helping you motivate students to choose responsible behavior.

Remember, the key is not the consequences themselves, but the inevitability that they will occur each time a rule is broken or a direction is not followed—not sometimes, not every now and then, but every single time.

Students will not respect your praise unless it is backed up with firm limits, and limits will be ineffective unless staying within those limits is backed up by praise.

Follow these guidelines to ensure that your use of disciplinary consequences will help students choose responsible behavior.

1. Provide consequences in a calm, matter-of-fact manner.

One of the benefits of a discipline hierarchy is that you always know how you will react to student misbehavior. Because you've *planned* how to deal with misbehavior, you will be able to give consequences calmly, without anger and with the assuredness that the consequence is both appropriate and fair.

> "Tom, this is the second time I've had to speak to you about calling out in class. You have chosen to wait after class for one minute."

Make sure that you emphasize that the consequence was the student's choice.

2. Be consistent. Provide a consequence every time a student chooses to disrupt.

As we have pointed out, it is the consistency of consequences that is the key to their effectiveness.

3. After a student receives a consequence, find the first opportunity you can to recognize positive behavior.

After a consequence has been given, teachers often continue to focus on that student's negative behavior—just waiting for the student to "act up" again. This may be a natural response, but it does little to encourage a student to choose more appropriate behavior.

Don't look for negative behavior. Instead, take the first opportunity to recognize the student's *appropriate* behavior. Your role in providing behavioral guidance to your students (not punishment) means that you must communicate the high expectations you have for each student's success.

Again, use discretion in how you recognize a student for appropriate behavior. Sometimes a simple smile or thumbs up from across the room can convey as much as a verbal acknowledgment.

4. Provide an "escape mechanism" for students who are upset and want to talk about what happened.

After receiving a consequence, students will often want you to stop what you are doing and listen to their side of the story.

The following "escape mechanisms" will let students diffuse their anger and "get something off their chest" without disrupting the rest of the class:

- Have the student write you a note that you will discuss with him or her after class or when you have a break in the lesson.

- Use a notebook to record misbehavior that allows space for students to write their comments.

- Have students keep a daily journal or diary in which they can record any comments.

5. When a student continuously disrupts, "move in" or "move out."

There may be times when a student will continue to disrupt even after he or she has been given a warning or a consequence. In these situations, a technique called "moving in" (see Cue Card #9 on the next page) will often effectively stop disruptive behavior.

Keep in mind that by providing consequences calmly and consistently, you will effectively help most students choose responsible behavior and stop most disruptive behavior in your classroom. In spite of these efforts, however, there are going to be some cases in which students will challenge your authority and confront you. When a student tries to manipulate you or argue with you, you must stay in charge and refocus the conversation. Refer to the refocusing technique on Cue Card #10 for specific guidelines.

Refer to pages 169-186 of the revised Assertive Discipline text for sample scenarios demonstrating teachers effectively using consequences in a variety of teaching situations.

"Moving In"

Many times physical proximity is all that is needed to help calm down a student and stop the disruptive behavior. Here's an effective technique to use when a student is being disruptive in class:

1 Move close to the student.

Walk over to the student. Get close. Show your concern and in a quiet, firm manner let the student know that his or her behavior is inappropriate.

2 In a caring manner, remind the student of the consequences received so far, and what will happen next if the misbehavior continues.

"Laurie, I am concerned that your behavior today is going to result in consequences that you don't really want. You've been doing well all this week. I'm proud of the work you've accomplished and I'd like to see it continue. Now you've received a warning and two consequences. One more disruption and I will be calling your parents tonight. Do you understand?"

Note: Do not "move in" on more than one student at a time.

With some students, "move out."

With some students, it is more appropriate to "move out" of the classroom to speak to the student. With these students, removing the audience of peers may increase the effectiveness of your limit-setting efforts.

When you "move out," remember to:

• stay calm.

• avoid arguing with the student.

• recognize the student's feelings.

Note: Do not "move" an older student out in front of the the class. Either step outside or quietly move to the side of the classroom. It is important that these students save face.

CUE CARD # 9
© 1992 Lee Canter & Associates

ASSERTIVE DISCIPLINE *in Action!*

Refocusing an argumentative conversation

When a student starts arguing with you, you must stay in charge. Do not get involved in an argument. Do not let the student pull you into a pointless exchange. Instead, stay in control, refocus the conversation and help get the student back on task.

Here's what to do:

- Stay calm.

- State what you want: "I want you to sit down and do your assignment."

- Preface your statement of want by expressing understanding for the student.

- Repeat your statement of want a maximum of three times. If the student still argues, let the student know that he or she will receive a consequence.

Here's an example of a teacher using the refocusing technique with a disruptive student:

Teacher: *(calmly, but firmly)* Debra, I want you to sit down and get to work on your assignment.

Debra: It's almost done. I'll finish it tonight. I have to talk to Carrie about our report for Mr. Johnson's class. We'll be quiet. We won't bother anyone.

Teacher: I understand, Debra, but you need to sit down and do your work for this class.

Debra: But I need to talk to Carrie. It's important. Why are you making such a big deal out of this?

Teacher: Debra, I see that you're upset, but sit down and begin your work.

Debra: I'm just trying to get my work done; it's due tomorrow.

Teacher: Debra, if you do not get to work immediately, you and I will call your mother during lunch. The choice is yours.

CUE CARD # 10

Difficult Students

Consistent use of the classroom management skills presented in the first part of this workbook will enable most teachers to teach 90 to 95% of their students to choose responsible behavior.

The remaining 5 to 10%—the difficult students you sometimes encounter—are the focus of this section in which we will cover four aspects of dealing successfully with difficult students:

- One-to-One Problem-Solving Conferences

- Using Positive Support to Build Positive Relationships

- Developing an Individualized Behavior Plan

- Getting Support from Parents and Administrators

One-to-One Problem-Solving Conferences

A one-to-one problem-solving conference is a meeting between you and your student to discuss a *specific* behavior problem. The goal of this conference is not to punish but to listen to the student and give caring and firm guidance. This conference should be looked upon as a cooperative effort on the student's behalf.

How do you know when a one-to-one conference is needed?

Ask yourself, "If this were my child, would I want the teacher to sit down and work with her to help improve her behavior? Would I want the teacher to take the time and interest to show my child better options?"

If the answer is yes, then it is time to meet with the student.

Keep these guidelines in mind when conducting a one-to-one problem-solving conference:

1 Show empathy and concern.
First and foremost, let the student know that you are concerned and that you care about him or her. Let the student know that you are meeting not to punish but to help and offer guidance.

2 Question the student to find out why there is a problem.
Don't assume you know why the student is misbehaving. Ask questions.

"Did something happen today to get you so upset?"

"Are other students giving you a hard time?"

"Does the work in this class seem too difficult?"

"Is there something happening at home or in your neighborhood that you're concerned about?"

3 Determine what you can do to help.
Is there anything you can do to help solve the problem? There may in fact be a simple answer that you don't want to overlook.

For example:

- If a student is having trouble in class with another student, move his seat.

- If a disruptive student is seated at the back of the class, consider moving her forward.

- Contact the parents if you feel the student needs additional help and support from home.

- Increase your positive attention toward the student, not just your consequences. Look for the first praiseworthy behavior after the conference, offer words of praise and send a positive note home.

- A student may need academic help that you, a tutor or a peer study buddy may be able to provide. Make that help available.

4 Determine how the student can improve his or her behavior.
Ask the student for his or her input concerning ways to improve the problem behavior. Share ideas. Keep in mind that some students may not be willing or able to share their feelings about choosing different behavior. If this is the case, help them by pointing out more appropriate behavior.

5 Agree on a course of action.
Combine your input with the student's input and agree upon a plan of action you can both follow to improve the situation.

6 Clearly state to the student that you expect him to change his behavior.

At some point during the conference you must let the student know that you expect behavior to improve.

> "I'm going to work with you to solve this problem, Joey. You're a smart student and I know you can behave responsibly. But you have to remember that while you're in this class, there are to be no put-downs of other students. From now on, any time you put another student down you will be choosing to go directly to the assistant principal."

7 Summarize the conference. Show your confidence!

Wrap up the conference by summarizing what was said. Most important, end with a note of confidence.

> "I think we made a good start today, Joey. I know you can do better tomorrow. I'm glad we had this talk. If you should ever feel like talking again, just let me know. I want this to be a good year for you."

Keep in mind that adolescents do not want to be *told* what to do. They want to feel they have a say in how they choose to behave. Whenever possible, involve the student in discussing how he or she should change behavior. Listen carefully to the student's input and give credence to his or her thoughts.

> *Please refer to pages 207-216 of the Assertive Discipline text for examples of scripted one-to-one problem solving conferences.*

It's Your Turn

Use the Problem-Solving Conference Worksheet on page 112 as a guide for conducting the conference and as a record of what was accomplished at the conference. If parents need to be involved at a future date, you will have documentation of steps already taken to solve the problem.

PROBLEM-SOLVING CONFERENCE
WORKSHEET

Student's name _____ Date _____

1. Problem behavior the student is having (reason for conference):

2. Student input regarding problem (Why does the student think this problem is occurring?):

3. Steps the teacher can take to help solve the problem:

4. Actions the student can take to solve the problem:

5. Course of action agreed upon between teacher and student:

Follow up and Notes:

PROBLEM-SOLVING CONFERENCE
WORKSHEET

Student's name _____ Date _____

1. Problem behavior the student is having (reason for conference):

_____

_____

_____

2. Student input regarding problem (Why does the student think this problem is occurring?):

_____

_____

3. Steps the teacher can take to help solve the problem:

_____

_____

_____

4. Actions the student can take to solve the problem:

_____

_____

_____

5. Course of action agreed upon between teacher and student:

_____

_____

_____

_____

Follow up and Notes:

_____

_____

_____

_____

_____

Using Positive Support to Build Positive Relationships

The adolescent years are stressful. Students' lives are filled with constant change as they leave childhood behind and experience the tumultuous physical, psychological and social changes that mark the entry into adulthood.

The secondary teacher, therefore, fills a very special role in students' lives. Quite simply, the teacher is a guide through some of the most difficult years a young person will encounter. And for many students, their teachers are the most positive, caring role models they will have.

It is extremely important, then, that you make a special effort to establish positive relationships with difficult students—relationships that demonstrate your caring commitment to their success and well being. Show these students that you care about them as unique individuals and that you are deeply concerned about their behavior.

In order to successfully raise the self-esteem of a difficult student, you may have to go beyond your daily program of praise and positive reinforcement. Use special approaches and activities that enable you to reach out to those students on an individual basis to build a strong, positive relationship.

It's as simple as this: Treat students the way you would want your own child to be treated in school.

It's Your Turn

The following pages contain ideas for fostering and building positive relationships with difficult students.

Discover Your Students' Interests

In order to establish personal relationships with your students, you need to learn about their likes and dislikes, interests and goals. A Student Interest Inventory, taken at the beginning of the year, is a great way to learn more about each student. Explain to your students that this inventory will help you become better acquainted with each of them. Make this inventory (page 115) the first homework assignment of the year. Keep a supply of Student Interest Inventories on hand throughout the year to give to transfer students entering your classroom. The information you gather from this inventory could be the building blocks of a positive student/teacher relationship.

Turnabout is fair play!

Don't forget, students will want to know something about you, too. Create a Teacher Interest Inventory detailing your likes and dislikes, interests and goals. Distribute a copy of the completed inventory to each student. Encourage students to discuss the inventory with you. Use the reproducible on page 116. Getting to know each other will help you build trusting relationships with students.

Don't hesitate to communicate!

A friendly note from a caring teacher can really make a student's day. Strengthen the positive support you give to your students, especially those who need extra guidance from you this year, with the reproducible self-esteem building notes on pages 117-119. Use them to express warm wishes to students or to share a few words of encouragement or appreciation. A bit of unexpected recognition can be the perfect booster students need to continue good efforts.

Look for opportunities each day to mail or hand out the following notes to students:

Get-Well Note (page 117)

Being a teenager sick in bed is just not fun. Take a moment to brighten the day of an ailing student. Send home a get-well note to let the student know you are thinking about him or her and are looking forward to his or her return to class. Students will return to your classroom feeling a lot better—not only physically, but emotionally as well!

End-of-Term "Great Job!" Note (page 117)

Be sure that students leave your class with positive feelings and high self-esteem. At the end of the term or semester, fill in a note to recognize each student for a special quality, talent or noteworthy contribution. Your favorable remarks will let students know that you care.

Thank-You Notes (page 118)

"Thank you!" They're just two little words, but they can mean so much. Use the thank-you notes to express appreciation to students for their help, cooperation and thoughtfulness in class—or just to say thanks for being a neat kid. Your thoughtfulness will be welcomed and appreciated.

Mid-Summer "Just Wanted to Stay in Touch" Letterhead (page 119)

By the end of the year you will have worked hard all year long to help your students succeed academically and behaviorally. There are bound to be two or three students from each of your classes who would still benefit from your support and interest. Take the time to send a letter to these students just to let them know that you're thinking about them. Communicate the confidence you have in their future success.

Ideas for Building Positive Relationships

Build strong, positive relationships with difficult students by incorporating the simple, yet effective techniques found on Assertive Discipline Cue Card #11 into your daily routine. Keep this card handy as a reminder of the many ways you can make positive contact with all students, especially difficult ones, throughout the day.

Please refer to pages 217-226 of the Assertive Discipline text for additional suggestions for building positive relationships with students.

STUDENT INTEREST INVENTORY

Name _____

Brothers and Sisters
Name _____ Age _____
Name _____ Age _____
Name _____ Age _____
Name _____ Age _____

Special friends:

_____   _____   _____

_____   _____   _____

What I like to do most at home: _____

_____

These are my favorite hobbies: _____

_____

These are my favorites:
book: _____   TV show: _____
movie: _____   food: _____
singer: _____   song: _____

If I had one wish, I would want to: _____

_____

School would be better if: _____

_____

If I had a million dollars, I would: _____

_____

This is what one of my teachers did last year that I liked the most: _____

_____

This is what one of my teachers did last year that I liked the least: _____

_____

_____

TEACHER INTEREST INVENTORY

Name _____

Family (optional):

Spouse _____

Children (ages) _____

Brothers and sisters _____

What I like to do most at home: _____
_____
_____

These are my favorite hobbies: _____
_____
_____

This is my favorite book: _____

This is my favorite TV show: _____

This is my favorite movie: _____

This is my favorite performer: _____

If I had one wish, I would want to: _____
_____
_____

If I had a million dollars, I would: _____
_____

What I like best about high-school students: _____
_____

What I like best about teaching: _____
_____
_____

Why I became a teacher: _____
_____
_____

Hope You're Feeling Better!

Great Job!

Thanks!

Thank You!

Just wanted to stay in touch...

Ideas for Using Positive Support to Build Positive Relationships

• Greet your students at the door.

Start each day with a smile and a personal greeting—for each and every student. Stand at the door as your students enter the room and greet each student by name. "Good morning, Pete. Nice to see you, Cindy. Hi, Jeff, I like your new jacket!" This is an especially effective way to make personal, positive contact with those students who need your individual attention and caring words.

• Spend a few special minutes with students who need your one-to-one attention.

The most precious and valuable gift you can give difficult students is your undivided attention. Take a few minutes during class, during lunch or after school to talk with the student. Share information about yourself. Inquire about the student's feelings and concerns. Let that student know that you are there to offer assistance, understanding and a sympathetic ear when necessary.

• Make home visits.

One very effective way to gain insight into a student's behavior is to visit that student and his or her family at home. Getting acquainted on this neutral ground is a great way to build positive relationships with

students and their families. Prearrange a home visit with the family. At the meeting inquire about their concerns and goals for the school year. Share your plans.

• Make a phone call after a difficult day.

End a difficult day on a positive note by phoning a student with a positive message about tomorrow. Discuss any difficulties that occurred during the day. Get student input. Most important, your phone call should emphasize your confidence that these problems can be worked through and that tomorrow both of you can start fresh.

• Make a positive phone call when a student has had a good day.

What better way to let a student know that he or she is on the right track than by making a quick phone call to offer some well-earned words of praise. If the student isn't home, share the good news with parents and have them deliver the positive message later.

• Make get-well phone calls.

When a student is ill, pick up the phone and call to find out how the child is feeling. Both parents and student will appreciate your caring and concern.

CUE CARD # 11

Developing an Individualized Behavior Plan

When your general classroom discipline plan is not effective with a student, you'll need to establish an individualized behavior plan for him or her. Such a plan is designed to adapt the elements of your regular classroom discipline plan to meet the unique needs of a particular student.

An individualized behavior plan can help teach the student to behave responsibly and help you to develop the positive relationship with that student that so far may have been out of reach.

An individualized behavior plan includes:

- The specific behaviors expected of the student.

- Meaningful consequences to be imposed if the student does not choose to engage in the appropriate behavior.

- Meaningful positive recognition to be given when the student does behave appropriately.

Guidelines for developing an individualized behavior plan:

1 Determine the behavior(s) you expect from the student.

Select only one or two behaviors to work on at a time. Choose those that you believe are most important to the student's success. For example, if a student has a consistent problem with staying in his seat, the rule "Stay in your seat unless you have permission to get up" would be an appropriate behavior to target.

2 Decide on meaningful consequences.

Often you will find that a difficult student reaches the same consequence on the discipline hierarchy each day. For example, a student might reach the third step on the hierarchy every day and stay after class for two minutes on each of those days.

First disruption   Warning

Second disruption: One minute after class

Third disruption: Two minutes after class

Fourth disruption: Contact parents

Fifth disruption: Send to vice principal

Conclusion? It appears in this case that the student does not really mind staying after class all that much and thus the consequence is not effective.

If you look at it in another way, you will note that the student *always* stops short of the consequence that involves calling the parent. In this case the teacher can conclude that it may be effective to individualize this student's discipline plan so that the first time she disrupts, instead of a warning or staying after class, her parents are immediately contacted.

For example:

First disruption: Call parents

Second disruption: Send student to vice principal

> Note: It may be appropriate with some difficult students to provide consequences that are not on your regular classroom discipline hierarchy. It may be necessary, for example, to keep a student in at lunch or after school even though those consequences are not on your hierarchy.

Keep in mind that no matter what the consequence is, it must always be one that will be meaningful to the student and, as always, provided consistently each time the student chooses to misbehave.

3 Determine more meaningful positive recognition.

Your firmer, more meaningful consequences must always be balanced with increased positive recognition. As always, your positive recognition should begin with praise. Once you have implemented an individualized behavior plan, look for every opportunity to recognize the student's appropriate behavior. Make it a point to genuinely praise the student several times a day.

Back up your praise with other forms of positive recognition that you feel are appropriate, such as positive notes home, a positive phone call home or special privileges.

Keep parents informed.

A parent's involvement in an individualized behavior plan is critical. After all, it is likely that "Call parents" may be the first consequence given. Whenever you establish an individualized plan for a student, personal contact with the parent is vital. A phone call or face-to-face meeting is your best means of communicating the plan.

Here are the points you will want to cover in the meeting:

1. Emphasize to the parents that your goal in establishing the individualized plan is to help the student learn more responsible behavior that will allow him or her to succeed in school.

2. Explain the one or two behaviors that you are dealing with in the plan. Let the parents know why you have chosen to emphasize these behaviors.

3. Tell the parents what will happen the first time the student breaks one of these rules. Explain why you have chosen these "more meaningful" consequences.

4. Tell the parents what will happen the second time a rule is broken.

5. Ask if the parents have any questions regarding the use of consequences in the individualized plan.

6. Now, explain the positive recognition you will give the student when he or she behaves appropriately. Reiterate the importance of reinforcing the student's efforts with consistent praise and other forms of recognition. Let the parents know that you are genuinely committed to the child's success.

7. Tell the parents that you will provide a regular update to keep them informed of their child's progress. (In most cases, since parent contact will be part of the revised hierarchy, parents will hear if there's a problem. However, it's just as important to give a call or send a note when the student does behave appropriately.) Emphasize the importance of parents following through at home with positive reinforcement of their own. If appropriate, give parents a copy of the student's individualized behavior plan.

Note: It is important that an individualized behavior plan be handled with sensitivity and caring. This is not a punitive effort; it is a plan tailor-made to meet a particular student's needs. Parents need to understand that this is a positive and proactive step, the goal of which is to help their child reach his or her potential. Let your words and attitude communicate this goal.

It's Your Turn

Use the Individualized Behavior Plan form on page 123 to help prepare and record a student's individualized plan.

The individualized behavior plan should be presented to the student in a firm but empathetic manner. Difficult students need your assurance that you care, that you are there to help and that the disruptive behavior is not in their best interests.

Refer to pages 233-234 of the revised Assertive Discipline text for a sample script for presenting an individualized behavior plan to a student.

INDIVIDUALIZED BEHAVIOR PLAN

Student's name _____ Date _____

These are the rules that _____ is expected to follow as part of this Individualized
Behavior Plan:

_____

_____

_____

These are the consequences _____ will choose to receive if he/she does not
comply with the rules:

First disruption: _____

Second disruption: _____

This is the positive recognition _____ will receive when he/she behaves
appropriately.

_____

_____

_____

_____

_____

Teacher's signature   Date

Notes or comments:

_____

_____

_____

_____

_____

_____

_____

_____

_____

_____

Getting the Support You Need from Parents and Administrators

In Section One you learned the importance of sharing your discipline plan with parents and with your administrator. These are important proactive measures that will help ensure that you get their support when you need it.

Keep these additional guidelines in mind as the year progresses and as behavior problems arise:

When a problem arises, take steps to deal with it on your own before asking for help.

Whenever appropriate, you should attempt to handle a student's disruptive behavior on your own before you speak to the parents or administrator about the situation. Both will want to know what actions you have taken to help the student. Assure them that you have already attempted to solve the problem on your own.

Remember, your goal is to teach the student to make good behavioral choices. If you involve parents or the administrator too soon, you are not allowing the student the opportunity to change his or her own behavior.

Document a student's behavior, and the steps you have taken to handle it.

Whenever you do contact parents or an administrator about a problem, you will need accurate anecdotal documentation detailing when the problem has occurred and what steps you have taken to deal with it. Documentation strengthens your position as a professional and communicates clearly to parents that these problems do exist.

Your anecdotal record should include the following information:

- Student's name

- Date, time and place of incident

- Description of the problem

- Actions taken by the teacher

For example:

Name: Jerome Hawkins

Date: 4/24/92

Problem: At 10:15 in English Lit class, Jerome tossed a baseball across the room to Evan.

Actions taken: Sent Jerome to the detention room for the rest of the period.

Keep these guidelines in mind when documenting problems:

Be specific. Keep away from vague opinions. Your statements should be based on factual, observable data.

Be consistent. Document problems each time they occur. Repeated occurrences may show a pattern and be helpful in solving the problem.

It's Your Turn

Use the reproducible documentation cards on page 125 to record anecdotal data about a student's behavior. Consider duplicating the cards on index stock for added durability. Fold in half with name facing forward.

Student _____ **Phone #** _____

Parent's Name _____ **Work #** _____

Parent's Name _____ **Work #** _____

•Date _____ **Time** _____ **Place** _____

Description of Problem/Incident: _____

_____

Action Taken: _____

•Date _____ **Time** _____ **Place** _____

Description of Problem/Incident: _____

_____

Action Taken: _____

< told here >

•Date _____ **Time** _____ **Place** _____

Description of Problem/Incident: _____

_____

Action Taken: _____

•Date _____ **Time** _____ **Place** _____

Description of Problem/Incident: _____

_____

Action Taken: _____

Student _____ **Phone #** _____

Parent's Name _____ **Work #** _____

Parent's Name _____ **Work #** _____

•Date _____ **Time** _____ **Place** _____

Description of Problem/Incident: _____

_____

Action Taken: _____

•Date _____ **Time** _____ **Place** _____

Description of Problem/Incident: _____

_____

Action Taken: _____

•Date _____ **Time** _____ **Place** _____

Description of Problem/Incident: _____

_____

Action Taken: _____

•Date _____ **Time** _____ **Place** _____

Description of Problem/Incident: _____

_____

Action Taken: _____

Behavior Documentation Cards

Getting Support from Parents When a Problem Arises

How do you know when you should contact a parent about a problem? Some situations are very clear: severe fighting, extreme emotional distress, a student who refuses to work or turn in homework. Don't think twice about involving parents when these situations occur.

What about the day to day instances that may not be so obvious? If you are uncertain about contacting a parent, use the "Your Own Child" test. This test will put you in the position of the parent, and help clarify whether or not parental help is called for.

The "Your Own Child" Test

1. Assume you have a child of your own the same age as the student in question.

2. If your child was having the same problem in school as that student has, would you want to be called?

3. If the answer is yes, call the parent. If the answer is no, do not call the parent.

Before you pick up a phone or meet with parents, you need to outline what you are going to say. These notes will help you think through and clarify the points you want to make. Having the notes in front of you while you're speaking will help you communicate more effectively.

It's Your Turn

Assertive Discipline Cue Card #12 lists all the points you'll want to cover when contacting a parent about a problem. Reproduce and laminate this Cue Card and keep it available for reference. Use the reproducible planning sheet on page 128 to help both prepare for your meeting and to record pertinent data from the meeting.

Contacting Parents About a Problem

Follow these steps when contacting a parent about a problem:

1. Begin with a statement of concern.

Let the parent know that you care about the student.

2. Describe the specific problem and present pertinent documentation.

Explain in specific, observable terms what the student did.

3. Describe what you have done.

Explain exactly how you have dealt with the problem so far. Make sure that the parent is aware of the steps you have already taken to solve the problem.

4. Get parental input on the problem.

Listen carefully to what the parent has to say. Here are some questions you may want to ask:

"Has your child had similar problems in the past?"

"Why do you feel your child is having these problems at school?"

"Is there something (divorce, separation, siblings, a move) going on at home that could be affecting your child's behavior?"

5. Get parental input on how to solve the problem.

Parents may have a good idea that could help solve a specific problem.

Ask for input, and listen carefully to the responses.

6. Tell the parent what you will do to help solve the problem.

You've already explained what you have previously done. Let the parent know exactly what specific actions you are going to take now.

7. Explain what you need the parent to do to solve the problem.

Clearly and carefully explain specifically what you would like the parent to do.

8. Let the parent know you are confident that the problem can be worked out.

Wrap up the conversation or meeting on a positive note. Express your confidence in working together.

9. Tell the parent that there will be follow-up contact from you.

The parent needs to know that you are going to stay involved. Provide this reassurance by giving a specific date for a follow-up call or note.

10. Recap the conference.

Clarify all agreements. Restate and write down what you are going to do and what the parent is going to do. Keep this information in your files.

CUE CARD # 12

PARENT CONTACT WORKSHEET

Guidelines for an initial phone call or conversation about a problem

Student's name _____ Date of call or meeting _____

Parent or guardian _____

Home phone # _____ Work phone # _____

In the spaces below write the important points you will cover with the parents, and points made during the meeting or conversation.

1. Begin with a statement of concern. _____

_____

2. Describe the specific problem (state in observable terms). _____

_____

3. Review what you have already done to solve the problem. _____

_____

4. Get parental input on how to solve the problem. Record parent comments. _____

_____

5. Present your solutions to the problem.

What you will do: _____

_____

What you want the parent to do: _____

_____

6. Express confidence once again in your ability to solve the problem.

7. Arrange for follow-up contact.

Notes _____

_____

_____

_____